The Traditional Chinese State in Ming Times (1368-1644)

The Traditional Chinese State in Ming Times (1368–1644)

CHARLES O. HUCKER

明代政治考

THE UNIVERSITY OF ARIZONA PRESS
TUCSON, ARIZONA

First printing 1961
Second printing 1963
Third printing 1964
Fourth printing 1966
Fifth printing 1968
Sixth printing 1970
Seventh printing 1972

THE UNIVERSITY OF ARIZONA PRESS

Copyright © 1961
The Arizona Board of Regents
All Rights Reserved
Manufactured in the U.S.A.

I.S.B.N. -0-8165-0093-2
L.C. No. 61-15391

For Myrl

FOREWORD

For more than twelve years I have focused my research activities on the study of Chinese government during the Ming period. Undoubtedly, a great compendium on this subject would be very welcome, but what follows is obviously not so ambitious a work. Neither can it be called an objective summary of all that modern scholarship has unearthed about Ming government. It is, rather, a highly interpretive distillation, in general and untechnical terms, of what I personally understand the Ming state system to have been. Whatever its faults, I hope it may be of some use both to students of traditional China and to students of comparative government.

In its original, only slightly different form, this essay was prepared as a contribution to a conference on political power in traditional China that was held at Laconia, New Hampshire, in September, 1959, under the auspices of Harvard University. To the participants in that conference, and especially to Professor Frederick W. Mote of Princeton University, I am indebted for many helpful criticisms, though I must necessarily bear full responsibility for any remaining shortcomings in the presentation.

I am very grateful to President Richard A. Harvill of The University of Arizona and to the Carnegie Corporation of New York for making this publication financially possible and to Dr. Jack L. Cross and his associates of The University of Arizona Press for making it physically attractive.

Charles O. Hucker

Tucson, Arizona

THE TRADITIONAL CHINESE
STATE IN MING TIMES
(1368–1644)

INTRODUCTION

One of mankind's most durable creations passed out of existence when old China's imperial system of government was submerged under a tide of republicanism in the early years of the present century. No other government that persisted into the twentieth century could claim comparable longevity; for its history as an institutional system stretched back almost unbroken through dynastic changes, foreign invasions, and social and cultural upheavals into the third century before Christ. In the long perspective of history, moreover, it is probable that no government ever served its people more effectively as a guardian of social stability, territorial integrity, and national dignity. Despite its rapid and complete deterioration at the end, the Chinese — Nationalist and Communist alike — have not ceased recalling its glories with a wistful nostalgia, and many have consistently lamented its passing.

Historians and political scientists of the Western world increasingly share this interest in the old system, in part because of its remarkable durability but principally because they have come to recognize in it a unique case in the human experience of government. China's imperial government was like no other — in its ideological foundations, in its institutional apparatus, in its personnel practices, or in its administrative processes. It left the Chinese people a heritage that gives a distinctive cast to their political thinking and their political institutions of the present day.

The purpose of this essay is to describe the traditional Chinese state as it existed and functioned during the period of the Ming dynasty (1368–1644). It would be too much to say that the old regime was at its best in Ming times. But the nomadic pressures that culminated in the Mongol conquest had ebbed away, and the disruptions attendant upon the Manchu conquest and the impact of the modern West were yet to appear. Imperial China was enjoying one of the most notably tranquil interludes of its history, and its long-maturing governmental system was having as good an opportunity as it ever had to function and develop in normal conditions.

This Ming government, like any government, was several things. In simplest terms, perhaps, it was an assortment of agencies or offices linked together into a distinctive organizational structure. From another point of view, it was a conglomeration of diverse groups of people in a distinctive pattern of relations to one another. It was also a complex of ideas — attitudes and values that manifested themselves as distinctive administrative practices. Considered from any of these points of view, it was probably the most elaborate and sophisticated governmental system existing in the world in its time.

ORGANIZATIONAL STRUCTURE OF THE MING GOVERNMENT[1]

Structurally, the Ming government was an institutional pyramid, unitary in over-all organization and centralized in operational control. At the vertex was a hereditary emperor in whom sovereignty resided, ensconced in a vast palace at the national capital (Nanking 1368–1420, Peking 1421–1644). The pyramid under him had three faces, so to speak: one hierarchy of agencies for civil administration, another for military administration, and a third providing a uniquely Chinese type of censorial surveillance over all. Each hierarchy culminated in agencies of the central government and each was also represented in the thirteen provinces into which China proper was divided for administration in Ming times. At each level, from top to bottom of each hierarchy, the principal officials were appointed representatives of the crown.

The civil administration hierarchy was the most elaborate of the three. In the early years of the Ming dynasty it was dominated at the top by a Secretariat, whose two Chief Councilors served as dual prime ministers. But in 1380, the secretariat superstructure was abolished, and thereafter civil administration at the top level was fragmented among six formerly subordinate Ministries, independent of one another and differentiated by functional responsibilities: Ministries of Personnel, of Revenue, of Rites, of War, of Justice, and of Works. Executive coordination now came to be provided in some measure, but less formally than before, by a newly created Grand Secretariat, consisting of several Grand Secretaries who nominally had no administrative authority but whose prestige and influence grew throughout the Ming period. The six Ministries, however, officially remained the core of the civil administration in the central government.

Associated with the Ministries in the national capital were numerous subsidiary agencies and a few important organs with autonomous status. Among the latter were an Office of Transmission serving as a central message center, a Hanlin Academy engaged in literary and scholarly production under crown auspices, a Directorate of Astronomy, a Directorate of Parks, an Imperial Academy of Medicine, a National University, and a supreme appellate tribunal for criminal cases called the Grand Court of Revision.

Channels for routine civil administration led down from the Ministries to Provincial Administration Offices in the various provinces and thence, successively, down to prefectures, subprefectures, and counties. But here, too, a supervisory superstructure came to be imposed on the regular establishment. This consisted of special delegates from the throne, of two sorts: (1) Grand Coordinators in the separate provinces and strategic frontier zones, serving virtually as provincial governors; and (2) Supreme Commanders assigned to larger regions, including as many as five provinces, to coordinate activities on a large scale in times of crises, especially military.

Both types of supervisors were officially temporary commissioners, but from the middle of the fifteenth century on, both tended to become regular components of the governmental system.

At the provincial and local level, too, the civil administration included numerous special establishments such as revenue agencies, granaries and storehouses, schools, and manufactories, some of which were subordinate to the regular provincial and local authorities and some of which were responsible directly to the Ministries in the central government.

The military hierarchy originally culminated in a unitary Chief Military Commission at the capital, but this was abolished in 1380 along with the Secretariat. Thenceforth military administration was fragmented among five coordinate Chief Military Commissions, counterparts of the mutually independent Ministries in the civil administration, but differentiated from one another on the basis of territorial control rather than function. Each Chief Military Commission thus had administrative jurisdiction over several Regional Military Commissions, which existed in all provinces and, additionally, in three vital defense areas along China's northern frontier. The Regional Commissions, in turn, had jurisdiction over garrison units known, in descending order of rank, as guards, battalions, and companies. Such garrisons existed throughout the empire but were most numerous at the frontiers.

The censorial hierarchy has had no counterpart outside the Chinese world. Traditional Chinese censorship was not a police activity of the familiar Western variety.

It was an elaborately organized and highly systematized effort by the government to police itself or, in the Chinese term, to "rectify administration." The aim of such censorship was threefold: (1) to ferret out and make known all violations of administrative regulations and public policy, (2) thereby to purge the government of incompetence and malfeasance, and (3) consequently to help maintain a governmental tone, so to speak, that accorded as closely as possible with the Chinese ideal. Its instrument was a special hierarchy of governmental officials who had no principal duties other than to provide routine surveillance over activities at all levels of administration and, in consequence of their surveillance, to impeach wayward personnel and recommend changes in governmental operations.

In a structural sense, this hierarchy was not as closely integrated as the others. Its most prominent organ was a metropolitan Censorate, or Chief Surveillance Office, which was structurally on a level with, and administratively independent of, the Ministries and the Chief Military Commissions. Also, related to the Censorate by function but enjoying equal administrative autonomy, there was a group of six coordinate Offices of Scrutiny, also at the capital, which were named in the pattern of the Ministries as the Office of Scrutiny for Personnel, for Revenue, and so on. At its lowest level, the censorial hierarchy included Provincial Surveillance Offices, one in each of the thirteen provinces. These agencies were not under the direct administrative control of either the Censorate or the Offices of Scrutiny, nor did they control any lower-echelon agencies comparable to those that were responsible to the Provincial Administration Offices and the Regional Military Commissions.

PERSONNEL COMPONENTS OF THE GOVERNMENT

The sprawling governmental establishment of the Ming period was staffed by a personnel corps of diverse components and of enormous numbers. Though not extraordinarily large in proportion to China's population, it was undoubtedly the largest single body of state-supported functionaries in existence in the world at the time. It included the emperor and his clansmen, personal attendants in the imperial household, a privileged class of noblemen, civil service bureaucrats and their assistants, and a military corps of officers and soldiers.

The Ming Emperors and Their Clansmen

The imperial clan itself was not only the most prestigeful but was one of the largest components of the corps of governmental personnel.

Sixteen men successively occupied the imperial throne during the 277 years of the Ming dynasty. They bore the imperial title Huang-ti and are known in history principally by the temple names with which they were addressed posthumously in religious ceremonies: Grand Progenitor (T'ai-tsu, 1368–98), Benevolent Ancestor

(Jen-tsung, 1424–25), Filial Ancestor (Hsiao-tsung, 1487–1505), Martial Ancestor (Wu-tsung, 1505–21), and so on. Each is also commonly identified with the era name, chosen as an auspicious omen, that took effect on the first new year's day of his reign: for example, Eternal Contentment (Yung-lo, 1403–24) and Prosperous Tranquility (Chia-ching, 1522–66). A commoner of peasant origin, Chu Yüan-chang (T'ai-tsu), the leader of a nationalistic rebellion against Mongol dominance in China, founded this imperial line. The fifteen other Ming emperors were all his direct descendants, surnamed Chu.[2]

Ming emperors were unrestricted in the number of consorts they might take, and it was common for an emperor to have three or four principal wives concurrently. However, only one of these could at any one time bear the official designation of Huang-hou, or Empress, and all children borne by any of the imperial consorts were officially considered to be her offspring. The emperors on the whole were rather prolific. None was more so than T'ai-tsu, who spawned twenty-six sons and sixteen daughters. But one of his successors had nineteen children, one had eighteen, and two had seventeen. Only two seem to have died without issue.

Every son of a reigning emperor was invested as an imperial prince and received a substantial stipend from state funds.[3] One son, normally the eldest, was designated heir apparent at an early age and inherited the throne in the normal course of events. Others were not permitted to remain in the imperial palace after attaining maturity, but were sent out to reside in provincial estates with retinues of civil and military personnel numbering from three thousand to nineteen thousand. They bore titles deriving from ancient territorial designations, such as Prince of Ch'u and Prince of Yen. These princeships were perpetuated through the generations from eldest son to eldest son, and new ones appeared with the junior sons of each new emperor. At least sixty-one such imperial princeships were created under different emperors, but not all were perpetuated to the end of the dynasty.

Junior sons of imperial princes, of whatever generation of descent from imperial origin, all became princes of the second degree, and their titles and privileges were likewise perpetuated from eldest son to eldest son. A total of sixty-nine such second-degree princeships stemmed from one of T'ai-tsu's sons alone. So it went through the degrees of relationship: eldest sons inherited their fathers' ranks, and junior sons were invested with lesser and lesser titles of royalty and lesser and lesser privileges. But every male descendant of every Ming emperor in the male line, all bearing the imperial surname Chu, theoretically received some title of royalty and a corresponding emolument from state funds.

Descendants of emperors in the female line fared somewhat less handsomely. Imperial princesses themselves enjoyed magnificent weddings often involving tremendous state expenditures, and their husbands received honorific titles as consorts, and state emoluments. Daughters of imperial princes of whatever degree, who also bore the surname Chu, brought similar honors and privileges to their husbands, though these diminished as the relationship with the imperial throne widened. But the offspring of such imperial clanswomen, since they did not bear the surname Chu themselves, were not royalty. Sons sometimes inherited the fathers' consortships, but most often they had to be contented with less prestigeful appointments as ordinary military officers. Daughters seem to have enjoyed no special status whatsoever.

The imperial clan naturally grew in size as the years and generations went by. It has been estimated that by the end of the Ming period the number of living clansmen had swelled to one hundred thousand.[4]

Attendants in the Imperial Household

The imperial residence was a city in itself within the capital city, Peking. It included numerous pavilions and halls, ponds, and even an artificial hill, all enclosed within a wall more than two miles in circuit. Called the Forbidden City, it was reserved for the exclusive use of the emperor, members of his immediate family, and their resident personal attendants. The household staff was necessarily large, and it consisted solely of women and eunuchs.

Palace women[5] seem to have been selected for imperial service while very young, from among candidates regularly offered, singly or in groups, by families anxious to obtain court favor. They were expected to be pleasing in appearance and manner and of respectable origins. Once admitted to service they secluded themselves from the outside world, unless conferred as imperial gifts upon favored personages or pensioned off in old age. In the early years of the dynasty they were organized into seven different agencies specializing in various aspects of palace maintenance; but eunuchs gradually assumed their service duties, and after the 1420's their organization dwindled to a single Bureau of Apparel. The most favored of them become companions, entertainers, and mistresses of the emperors. Those who were especially pleasing gained recognition as imperial consorts or even as empresses.

Partly in fear of appearing extravagant, the founding emperor, T'ai-tsu, restricted the number of palace women to ninety-three. But the number grew, especially during the last century of the dynasty. One emperor of the succeeding Manchu line insisted that the Ming palace in the end had swarmed with nine thousand women.[6]

Palace eunuchs[7] were even more numerous. It was T'ai-tsu's intention that the eunuch staff should not exceed one hundred persons, but it did not remain at this low level. By the end of the fifteenth century eunuchs apparently numbered ten thousand; late in the sixteenth century they were regularly recruited in groups of more than three thousand at a time; and by the end of the dynasty it has been estimated their number had grown to more than seventy thousand.[8]

How eunuchs were recruited is not wholly clear. Although self-castration was prohibited by Ming law, men of low station and no prospects often sought this route to security and influence; emperors were moved to fulminate against the practice again and again throughout the dynasty. Perhaps more commonly, ambitious parents with the good fortune of having several sons sometimes offered one young boy for palace service. This was permitted by law; but whether such boys suffered castration before or after their acceptance for service is not clear. At all events, the eunuch staff seems to have been recruited and regularly replenished through voluntary action on the part of the candidates or their parents. Since castration was not a statutory punishment in Ming times, the staff could not have been maintained by judicial processes.[9]

As the number of eunuchs proliferated, so did the complex of agencies in which they were organized. The basic establishment consisted of twenty-four offices charged with various aspects of palace maintenance: the care of utensils, ceremonial equipment, apparel, stables, and seals; the management of granaries and storehouses of all kinds; the provision of fuel, foodstuffs, music, paper, and baths; the handling of documents; the upkeep of buildings and grounds; and the manufacture of textiles, art objects, and other craft goods. Eunuchs also supervised the palace treasury. The most prestigeful of all the eunuch agencies was the Directorate of Ceremonial, whose head was the unchallenged chief of the palace staff.

Eunuch attendants were also authorized for the households of imperial princes. It has consequently been estimated that the total of eunuchs in service throughout the empire by the end of the Ming period, including the estimated seventy thousand at the capital, may have approached one hundred thousand.[10]

The Nobility

The Ming nobility consisted of dignitaries holding the titles of duke, marquis, and earl, in descending order of rank.[11] They were not feudal aristocrats who enjoyed privileges and powers handed down from pre-Ming eras. They were appointees of the Ming emperors, they received stipends paid from state funds but no territorial grants, and they enjoyed their noble status at the pleasure of the emperors. Some could perpetuate their titles to descendants but others could not, depending upon the terms of the original investment.

Emperors utilized noble titles as rewards for those who had rendered extraordinary service to the throne. For the most part, they went to officers of the military corps who had given distinguished service in battle. Only rarely was an official of the civil service so honored. But a few noble titles also regularly went to the fathers or brothers of empresses, especially to those who were grandfathers or uncles of emperors-to-be; and occasionally even the relatives of favored eunuchs were ennobled. One relative of a notorious eunuch of the 1620's, as a matter of fact, was the recipient of the only new dukeship created after the middle of the fifteenth century. And one man was made an earl as a reward for his alchemical efforts to discover an immortality drug for the emperor Shih-tsung (1521–66).

Not counting titles that were conferred posthumously without inheritance rights, which thus were never borne by living men, there were created during the successive reigns of the Ming dynasty totals of twenty-one appointments as dukes, one hundred two appointments as marquises, and one hundred thirty-eight appointments as earls. Forty-five of these various appointments, mostly as earls, went to imperial in-laws and other palace favorites. More than half of all noble titles were not perpetuated beyond the original appointees, and few of the remainder were perpetuated for more than three generations.

The Civil Bureaucracy

Principal positions in both the civil and censorial hierarchies of the government, at all levels down to the county, were held by officials with civil service status comparable to that common in the Western world today.[12] Graded in eighteen ranks ranging from 1a at the top down to 9b, they received stipends from state funds and moved about from assignment to assignment in the governmental pyramid at the pleasure of the emperor. The prescribed total of civil service positions apparently grew from about fifty-four hundred in the early years of the dynasty to more than fifteen thousand in its latter years, probably fluctuating between ten thousand and fifteen thousand during most of the period.[13]

Status as a civil service official was highly coveted, and various avenues of recruitment existed. At the beginning of the Ming period, when there was a sudden need for numerous administrators, persons were recruited primarily through recommendations by existing officials. Shortly thereafter, when a government-supported network of schools had been created, men commonly entered the service following promotion from local schools to the National University at the capital and satisfactory completion of a study program there. From 1450 on, status as a special student at the National University — and thus a chance for ultimate civil service status — could be purchased by patriotic contributions to the government in times of military crises; and such status was occasionally conferred by imperial grace upon sons of men who had lost their lives in state service. Throughout the dynasty, also, a few men regularly gained admittance to the National University or directly to the civil service through inheritance privileges conferred as rewards upon high-ranking civil service officials.

Generally speaking, however, all these avenues of entry into the civil service were subsidiary ones, carrying little prestige. No one who owed his official status to purchase or inheritance ever rose out of the lowest service ranks. After the early years of the dynasty, furthermore, the recommendation system withered away and entry into the service through the school system had little esteem. During the latter two hundred years of the dynasty there was only one avenue of entry that could lead to a successful career. That was a sequence of public, competitive examinations.

Students in government schools and privately tutored scholars alike could qualify for these examinations. Provincial education intendants visited all counties once a year and certified all male citizens of proper scholarly attainment and of good moral character as Bachelors (*Hsiu-ts'ai*) — titles that must be renewed at intervals of not less than three years and that could be revoked at any time for improper conduct. Several privileges were accorded Bachelors, one of which was the right to participate in examinations conducted under imperial auspices at the various provincial capitals every third year. The provincial examinations were exhausting ones, covering three full days of writing spaced over a week. Those who passed were entitled Licentiates (*Chü-jen*) and given new privileges. Their success qualified them in turn to participate in an empire-wide metropolitan examination conducted at the national capital several months later, also every third year. This examination was still more difficult, and those who passed received still greater privileges and certification as Doctors (*Chin-shih*). In all, 24,874 doctorates were conferred in the ninety metropolitan examinations conducted during the Ming period, an average of two hundred seventy-six per examination. The smallest number of degrees granted at any examination was thirty-two; the largest, four hundred seventy-two.[14]

Rosters of all degree-holders were maintained by the Ministry of Personnel, which was in general charge of assignments in the civil service. Bachelors who obtained no higher degrees could not expect governmental appointments. Persons who got no farther than the Licentiate degree were eligible for assignments but seldom were able to move into the higher ranks of the service. A Doctor, however, was almost guaranteed an appointment and could expect, if all went well, to progress steadily up the ladder of civil service ranks and perhaps to emerge late in life among the greatest dignitaries of the realm as a Grand Secretary, a Minister or Vice-Minister, or a Censor-in-chief.

But progress in a civil service career was by no means automatic. Normal tenure in a specific position was nine years. During his tenure, each appointee was regularly evaluated and rated by his administrative superiors and by censorial investigators. At any time, on the basis of his merit ratings, he could be demoted or otherwise punished, transferred in grade, or promoted; and at the conclusion of his ninth year, if not before, his merit ratings determined what new nine-year appointment he would be given. Only officials who had consistently won superior ratings over many years in service could become eligible eventually for promotion into the highest ranks.

Associated with the executive-like civil bureaucrats at all levels of government were large numbers of lesser functionaries who performed clerical and technical tasks. Though locally recruited and not considered part of the civil service proper, they did have recognized governmental status roughly comparable to that of noncommissioned officers in a modern army. They were given periodic merit ratings, and after nine years of honorable performance they were eligible for promotion into the lower civil service ranks. The lesser functionaries greatly outnumbered the civil bureaucrats, perhaps exceeding one hundred thousand.[15]

The Military Corps

The military establishment[16] was at all times the largest personnel component of the Ming government. In the early years of the dynasty it included more than fifteen thousand officers and more than one million one hundred thousand soldiers; and in the late years the totals are reported to have grown to approximately one hundred thousand and four million, respectively.[17]

Military officers had ranks like those of the civil officials, ranging from 1a down only through 6b, and they experienced similar merit evaluations. But the military personnel system differed substantially from its civil service counterpart. The principal difference lay in its methods of recruitment. Generally speaking, the military service was a hereditary one. The positions to which military officers were appointed were of two main types: hereditary offices (those in the guards, battalions, and companies), which seem to have passed directly from father to son, and so-called circulating offices (those of higher rank), which were filled by special merit selections from among the holders of the hereditary offices. Before being certified for appointment to a hereditary office, the son of an officer had merely to demonstrate competence in such military techniques as riding and archery.

The pool of hereditary officers was supplemented after 1478 with officers recruited in open competitive examinations superficially comparable to the civil service examinations, leading to the military doctorate. But these examinations did little, apparently, to change the hereditary character of the military service and give it prestige comparable to that of the civil service, since they required only demonstrations of competence in military skills. Most candidates seem to have been sons of military officers who were not eligible for inheritance.

Like most of their officers, soldiers of the basic military establishment provided hereditary service. When they died or became over-aged, their families had to present replacements for them, generation after generation. In consideration of this burden, the state gave families of soldiers perpetual exemptions from many of the taxes and labor services that were levied on civilian families. Soldiers so obtained were garrisoned permanently in the guards, battalions, and companies scattered about the empire, where they trained and, at least theoretically, supported themselves by part-time farming on state lands specially set aside for their use. From these garrisons they were periodically rotated to special training divisions at the capital and, when occasion arose, were also rotated to tactical commands for frontier defense duty or campaigning.

The hereditary military establishment did not prove adequate for defense purposes in the late Ming years. The frontier forces had to be augmented and were finally almost superseded by auxiliaries lured or coerced into service for pay.

GOVERNMENTAL RELATIONS WITH SOCIETY AT LARGE

The pyramid-like institutional apparatus and the varied personnel corps of the Ming government completely dominated the Chinese world. This was one of the remarkable characteristics of China's traditional state system. There was no group or force in society that served as a countervailing influence against the government, so that the society was a single-centered rather than a multicentered one. In this society, ". . . the men of the government prevented the organizational consolidation of all non-governmental groups."[18] In the same sense that all roads in the West once led to Rome, so hierarchical social relationships bound the Chinese into a unitary national family, with all societal elements integrated under the governmental superstructure. Nothing was independent of the government. Society, nation, and state were therefore conceptually inseparable.

Non-Chinese

The world with which the Ming government was concerned contained more, of course, than merely the Chinese themselves. It also contained various groups of non-Chinese peoples, living mostly on the fringes of China proper, who were always potentially and sometimes actively hostile. China's experience of Mongol rule during the thirteenth and fourteenth centuries caused the Ming government to be especially aware of the threat posed by these outsiders; it was probably much more alert in this regard than its predecessors had been.

Ming tactics in dealing with the non-Chinese varied from time to time and from group to group. The founding emperor T'ai-tsu (1368–98) and his vigorous son Ch'eng-tsu (1402–24) tried to keep all foreigners, and especially the Mongols, in a state of cowed subjection by aggressive campaigning. Ch'eng-tsu even conquered Annam to the south and incorporated it for a time as a province of China proper, and he sent great fleets into Southeast Asia and the Indian Ocean to overawe principalities as far distant as the east coast of Africa. Subsequent rulers of the Ming line, however, did not maintain this early aggressive policy. They mounted elaborate military defenses along China's frontiers, and they undertook vigorous defensive campaigns whenever China proper was threatened by invasion — as it was often by the Mongols, occasionally by Japanese pirates, and ultimately by the Manchus. Shen-tsung (1572–1620) unhesitatingly sent Chinese forces to defend Korea from Japanese invasion in the 1590's, and earlier the Ming court had given some consideration to sending a punitive expedition against the Portuguese after Malacca fell to them in 1511. But, on the whole, the last two centuries of Ming rule were marked by a nonaggressive foreign policy verging on appeasement. Its aim was to incorporate foreigners as much as possible into the Chinese structure of authority by granting them prestigeful status and material benefits, and thus to neutralize their hostile potential.

Among the important non-Chinese with whom the Ming government dealt were primitive aboriginal peoples of several different ethnic varieties occupying parts of China's southwestern provinces, where they remain even today as minorities not wholly incorporated into the Chinese way of life. From time to time throughout the Ming dynasty, one or another group of these aborigines rose in rebellion; but, at least after the early Ming decades, they were kept generally pacified by laissez-faire treatment on the part of the government. Their tribal organizations were given designations comparable to those of the regular Chinese administration — prefectures, subprefectures, counties, and some others of special sorts; and Chinese-like official titles, some with civil and some with military connotations, were conferred automatically upon their hereditary chiefs. But, in general, they were allowed to live their tribal lives without interference. They were expected only to keep the peace; virtually no other demands were made on them.[19]

The pattern of relations was somewhat different for other groups: Mongols, Manchus, Turkic peoples of Central Asia, Koreans, Japanese, and various Southeast Asian peoples notably including Annamese and Burmese. The inhabitants of modern Manchuria and Inner Mongolia were organized into guards, battalions, and companies of the Chinese sort, under native officers dignified with Chinese military titles; and some regular Chinese military units were garrisoned among them for security purposes. But all other groups were allowed to exist in their traditional patterns. The Ming court recognized their de facto rulers — normally hereditary chiefs — as princes roughly equal in rank and prestige to Chinese princes, and a big brother-little brother relationship was assumed. The foreign princes were expected to accept investiture by the Ming emperor, to accept and utilize the Ming calendar as a symbol of vassalage, and to send periodic missions to Peking to offer homage and submit tribute. In exchange for these manifestations of submission and for keeping the peace, the foreign princes were promised military protection if they were challenged, were treated always with flattering ritual, were given generous gifts as tokens of the emperor's paternalistic affection and approval, and were permitted also to carry on very lucrative trade with China.[20] The advantages to foreign rulers apparently far outweighed the humiliating submissiveness that the system imposed on them: one Central Asian of Ming times reported that his investment in tribute was repaid more than sevenfold in gifts from the Chinese throne, not even counting trading profits.[21]

Modern Europeans, who first appeared on the Chinese scene in 1514, encountered mistrust and repression because they had no traditional place in this network of tributary relationships and because they had deservedly acquired reputations as trouble-makers. European missionaries, who won Chinese respect for their learning and gentility, finally got permission to travel inland; but traders were carefully restricted to small-scale activities along the south coast until the end of the Ming dynasty.[22]

The General Population

The Chinese population in Ming times was probably not much larger than it had been during the preceding thousand years. Census registers of the period show a fluctuation between fifty and sixty million persons. Unregistered persons of various categories must have swelled the total to about one hundred million by the seventeenth century, and perhaps to an even larger number.[23] The population consisted overwhelmingly of peasants, but there was nevertheless a notable degree of urban living. Urban prefectures with registered populations exceeding one hundred thousand were common in most regions. The capital prefecture of Peking reached a recorded high of 706,861 registrants; that of Nanking 1,093,620. The most populous prefecture of all, Su-chou in the vicinity of modern Shanghai, maintained a registration consistently in excess of two million persons.[24]

As in other periods of Chinese history, society consisted of closely-knit family units, to which individuals were entirely subordinate. The family was held together partly by ancestor worship, involving the concept that the family was an indefinitely-perpetuated corporation jealously watched over by the spirits of all its dead, and partly by a customary responsibility to society at large on the part of the family as a whole for the actions of all its members. In Ming China every man was indeed his brother's keeper. The patriarchal family head dominated family councils and controlled family property. His parental responsibility and authority were unquestioned, and his sway might extend over several related nuclear families comprising a locally-organized clan. He shielded his family or clan from and represented it before the outside world.

The horizons of this outside world, in the case of the ordinary Chinese family, lay within the county, rural or urban, in which it resided. As heaven is high, the proverb went, so the emperor is far away. It was therefore at the county level that the paterfamilias normally made his only contact with the imperial governmental apparatus, and the relationship here was essentially an extension in a new hierarchical dimension of that between the paterfamilias and his sib. That is, the magistrate's authority, like a parent's, was all-encompassing and for practical purposes unchallengeable.

Since the average registered population per county exceeded fifty thousand, however, the contact between government and people even at this level was not very close. Moreover, the relationship between magistrate and paterfamilias was not direct; for one of the governmental innovations of the Ming dynasty was the establishment of an elaborate organizational apparatus among the people at an intermediate level between the magistrate and the families of his jurisdiction. The government called upon the people to regulate their own affairs through this apparatus, and the result was a certain measure of local self-government.[25]

One kind of sub-county organization was a special tax-collection district comprising an arbitrarily delimited aggregation of lands the tax revenues from which amounted to a uniform unit of ten thousand bushels of grain. The head of one prosperous family within each district was designated collector of land taxes, and all the collectors within a given county served as fiscal intermediaries between the county magistrate and the population at large. But this arrangement persisted only until the latter part of the sixteenth century, when a more direct method of tax payment was instituted.

A more basic unit of sub-county organization was a "community" (originally *li*, later *pao*) comparable in some ways to a modern ward or precinct. Each community in theory consisted of one hundred ten neighboring households, rural or urban. Heads of the ten most prosperous households were designated community chiefs and served annual terms in rotation as representatives of the community in dealings with the county magistrate or, in tax matters, with the intermediary collector of land taxes. The remaining hundred households were subdivided into ten tithings *(chia)* of ten households each. In each tithing one household provided a tithing chief to represent his tithing to the community chief.

Each community functioned in accordance with a so-called community agreement, a sort of constitution for local self-government prepared by the members in a pattern prescribed by imperial edict. This provided for the communal management of all local affairs and especially for the settling of disputes by the community chief; for the magistrates chastened communities that could not resolve their own intra-community litigations. The community agreement also included an exhortation to all citizens, first promulgated by the emperor T'ai-tsu, to be filial and obedient to their parents, to be respectful to their superiors, to be harmonious within the community, to educate their sons and brothers, to be content each in his lot, and not to do evil.[26] The entire text of the agreement was read aloud at monthly community assemblies, and participants in the assemblies also recited an oath that they would preserve propriety and the law, would not permit coercion of the weak, would deal with lawlessness themselves within the community, would care for the poor, and would assist one another to bear the burdensome expenses of weddings and funerals.[27] The community was expected to maintain a community altar for religious ceremonies, a community school, and a community granary for charitable uses.

Through the community organization the government extracted what it wanted from the people. Taxes were an important part of its levies. But it also levied corvée labor services — for local militia forces; for work on large-scale construction projects on roads and waterways, irrigation systems, public buildings, and the like;

and to provide lictors, couriers, transport bearers, and menial flunkies of various sorts for the county governmental establishment.

Moreover, the community organization provided a method of maintaining peace and order without the establishment of government-supported police forces. Each community as a whole was a guarantor of the good conduct of all its members, and it could also be held responsible for derelictions in adjacent communities. Therefore, although the *li-chia* or *pao-chia* system was consonant with a pre-existing and always observable Chinese penchant for familial and communal cooperation, it seems essentially to have served as a system of mass control. "It is far easier to regard it as an extension of imperial control down to the lowest level than to think of it as a system of rural self-government."[28]

Special Groups and Classes

Since the Chinese have always excelled at organizing themselves, Ming society was more than a vast aggregation of families leagued together in tithings and communities of the sort just described. It also included special groups — for example, of religious and occupational sorts. These groups were by their very nature potential competitors of the government for the loyalty of large numbers of people, and the government consequently gave them close attention.

RELIGIOUS GROUPS

Religious groups were of special significance. Buddhism and Taoism, the only organized religions of the

Chinese tradition, shared complete dominance over the religious life of the Chinese beyond the sphere of state ritual and family-oriented ancestor worship. Their monasteries and nunneries were imposing features of the Ming landscape, and clerics were held in great popular esteem. The Jesuit visitor Matteo Ricci could not avoid observing, with shocked revulsion, the Buddhist and Taoist influences of the sixteenth and early seventeenth centuries. "In public squares, in villages, on boats, and through the public buildings," he reported of religious art, "this common abomination is the first thing to strike the attention of a spectator."[29]

Both Buddhism and Taoism had long histories of political influence, and especially of association with rebellious secret societies. The immediate predecessors of the Ming dynasty, the Mongol emperors of the Yüan dynasty (1260–1368), had been particularly subject to Buddhist influence, with unfortunate consequences for themselves and for the Chinese people; and their dynasty had fallen in the end to rebels fortified with religious zeal. The Ming founder, T'ai-tsu, had himself come to power through a career as Buddhist neophyte, then mendicant monk, and finally coordinator of secret societies with Buddhist, Taoist, and even Manichaean backgrounds, and the dynastic name Ming, "Brightness," was chosen as a religious symbol.[30] There was no want of clear evidence, therefore, of the potential power of the religious orders.

Well aware of the danger, T'ai-tsu, on taking the throne, established restrictions which checked religious influence on politics so effectively that the Ming period was probably less troubled by religiously inspired disturbances than any other of the imperial era. All Ming emperors showed great public respect for religion, and some gave excessive patronage to individual monks. But, except for an inconsequential uprising of the Buddhist White Lotus Society in 1622,[31] the sects gave little cause for alarm.

This pacification of the religious orders was accomplished principally by their incorporation into the state governmental apparatus. Patriarchs of the two orders were appointed nominal heads of a Central Buddhist Registry and a Central Taoist Registry at the capital, and the leaders of local religious establishments were named to comparable offices at the prefectural, subprefectural, and county levels. All were supervised by the Ministry of Rites, and the religious leaders were held responsible to the Ministry for the activities of their orders. They were required regularly to examine all monks, to issue government certificates to those who qualified, and to dismiss from the orders all those who were not genuine practitioners of the doctrines. Other repressive controls were also employed. The size of religious communities was severely restricted. The number of either Buddhist or Taoist monks and nuns in any one county, for example, was limited by statute to twenty. A further restriction prevented the orders from recruiting monks before the age of forty and nuns before the age of fifty. Thus, although it is improbable that all these restrictions were rigidly enforced, the Ming government undertook at all times to keep the religious establishments under firm control.[32]

THE BUSINESS CLASS

Mercantile and industrial groups did not pose a comparable political threat to the government, but their activities were also carefully regulated. As at all times in China's past, agriculture was considered the only honorable profession except for governmental service, and profit-seeking adventures in commerce and industry were regularly denounced by Ming rulers as being exploitative and corrupting cancers in society. Although it was recognized that they provided a service of some social utility, persons who engaged in private business ventures were consistently discriminated against in such ways as to discredit them in public esteem. They were forbidden to wear clothing of better grade silk, for example.[33]

Merchants and industrialists customarily organized themselves into local guilds identified by the types of commodities or services with which they dealt, and the guilds largely determined the conditions of trade in their spheres. But governmental inspectors regularly checked on the accuracy of scales and measures in mercantile establishments and on the quality of goods produced in craft establishments, and they kept records of commodity prices. Anyone whose goods were of less than acceptable quantity and quality or whose prices were deemed exorbitant was subject to punishment by the government. A monthly inventory tax was collected from all businesses, and a kind of domestic customs duty was levied on all goods in transit.[34]

Each guild had a guild chief certified by the government who was, in some measure not wholly clear, responsible to the government for the conduct of the guildsmen.

Boat traders were similarly organized under harbor chiefs. Traders could travel about only with passports issued by the government, and every guild chief and harbor chief was required to present to the government each month a complete accounting of the identities and activities of all visiting traders.[35] In order to prevent too complete monopolization of trade by resident guild chiefs, the government in some cities established its own trading warehouses, from which visiting merchants might sell directly to retail outlets.[36]

The major factor in repressing the growth of business interests was not these supervisory restrictions on the part of the government, however; it was active governmental monopolization of the production and distribution of various commodities. This monopolization had two aspects. On the one hand, manufactured goods that were consumed by the government itself were, generally speaking, produced by the government. Peking abounded with armories, textile factories, metalwork shops, leatherwork shops, saddlery shops, paint shops, apparel factories, wineries, and the like, all operated by the Ministry of Works or by eunuchs, to provide the court and the central government with their commodity needs. In addition, there were government-operated weaving and dying establishments at Nanking, Su-chou, Hang-chou, and other great cities, and a famous pottery factory at Ching-te-chen in Kiangsi province. Since the government was by far the largest single consumer of many commodities, its reliance on its own producing agencies deprived private businessmen of one of their best opportunities for enrichment.

On the other hand, the government exercised monopolistic control over the production and distribution of commodities that were essential to the population at large and susceptible to private monopolistic exploitation. Principal commodities of this type were salt and iron, which were readily available only in limited areas but were required throughout the empire. Production and distribution of these goods were directly controlled by special agencies established at appropriate places under the supervision of the central government.[37] Each producing area was assigned a production quota and workers turned over their total product to the government. The governmental agencies in turn sold to private merchants according to quotas, and inspection stations throughout the empire seized as contraband any monopoly goods that were not accompanied by appropriate government certificates. In times of surplus, the government did not hesitate to impose impractically large quotas upon unhappy merchants. At times, too, it required merchants to earn coveted salt-purchase certificates by delivering foodstuffs to distant frontier military garrisons.

Workers in the government's industrial establishments and in the government-monopoly enterprises were generally hereditary laborers and craftsmen. Like the military families that provided sons for army service, they were considered a class apart from the general civilian population. They were organized under patriarchal foremen or masters who contracted for their services with the government and, like tithing chiefs or community chiefs, were totally responsible for their conduct. Moreover, each master was a guarantor of the good conduct of his neighboring masters.[38]

These monopolistic and repressive tactics of the government prevented the rise of a tycoon class in Ming China. But they did not prevent the corruption of public and especially governmental morality. The evidence suggests that mercantile wealth became steadily more esteemed during the Ming period and that customs became increasingly extravagant, to the detriment of the rather puritanical agrarian values espoused by the government. Specifically, imperial clansmen, imperial in-laws, and eunuchs by the latter years of the Ming period were using their privileged positions to dabble exploitively in commercial enterprises and to corrupt the administration of state monopolies for their own benefit.[39]

THE GENTRY

Of greater social significance in Ming times than either religious or business groups was the so-called gentry, a non-laboring class whose members were popularly considered persons of quality. The status was not self-perpetuating. Membership fluctuated from generation to generation in accord with the fluctuating fortunes of individual families. But the class persisted, and it monopolized local wealth and local leadership in such a way as to dominate economic and political life in the villages and towns.

From the point of view of economics, members of the gentry were landlords, money lenders, and sometimes investors in and proprietors of business establishments. To some extent they were ruthless exploiters of the peasant population.[40] Since there was always a shortage of capital, they were able quite legally, by contract, to impose crushing rents and interest rates, and their collection agents often bullied their clients mercilessly. Recurring natural disasters enabled them to expand their holdings at the expense of bankrupt mortgagees, and poor families often delivered themselves and their properties into gentry possession, in a form of contractual serfdom, to gain protection from irregular exploitation, private or governmental. By late Ming times it was not uncommon for large gentry families to have several thousand indentured clients of this sort, some of them little more than slaves.[41] Some gentry families came to possess little baronies, in which they extorted private tolls on travelers and on merchandise in transit.[42]

But the gentry families were by no means completely oppressive in their economic domination of the local scene. Gentry relations with the peasantry were close and personal ones and were thus tempered with paternalistic concerns. Reliance on gentry benevolence was often the only resource available to the poor. Moreover, gentry families recognized that being persons of quality involved a certain measure of community service, and they regularly contributed schools, roads, bridges, temples, irrigation works, entertainments, charitable institutions, and other benefits to their communities.

In the political sphere gentry domination was based upon monopolization of almost all local contacts with the imperial government. It was members of the gentry who mediated between the government and the people as community chiefs and district collectors of land taxes —

positions that gave their local power a semi-governmental sanction. Moreover, gentry members were the only Chinese, generally speaking, who had sufficient wealth and leisure to educate themselves, so that the gentry formed the pool of literati from which the government obtained its non-hereditary administrative personnel. The Chinese term that is traditionally rendered "gentry," as a matter of fact, literally denotes degree-holders, and the association between the local elite and government service was so close that the existence of a non-degree gentry group of large-scale landlords is questionable.[43]

As educated men, gentry members enjoyed a camaraderie with governmental officials based on common interests, and they were the natural informants about local customs and attitudes for officials who, by rule, were never assigned to posts in their own home provinces. Gentry dominance over the local peasantry was inevitably enhanced by these social contacts with officialdom. It was further facilitated by the success of gentry sons in civil service examinations. For one thing, status as a degree-holder automatically gave one's family important exemptions from governmental tax and corvée obligations, and it incidentally qualified one to augment the family's wealth by salaried service in the county governmental establishment and by earning tutorial fees. Success in the higher examinations brought possible appointments in the civil service itself, with even greater monetary returns in salaries, gifts, and irregular enhancements of income from various sources. The higher one rose in governmental service, the more his relatives back home were able to capitalize on their prestigeful connections by practicing various forms of exploitation without serious hindrance. So many opportunities for the acquisition of wealth came with degree-holding status that literati possibly begat landlords to a greater extent than landlords begat literati. Or, at least, it appears probable that constant renewal of literati privileges by examination successes generation after generation was necessary to perpetuate wealth and large-scale landownership.

The gentry was a social and economic class rather than a formally organized group in society. It was locally-based and family-oriented. Gentry families cooperated with one another in varying combinations to achieve specific community goals, and those of any one region tended to become linked by marriages. Moreover, members of the gentry throughout China seemed to have a community consciousness based on similar backgrounds, similar status, and similar interests. But the gentry had no formal organizations comparable, for example, to the guilds of the commercial and industrial classes. It always remained an unorganized class of independent large families.

The nearest approach to formal inter-family organization among the gentry was association of literati in literary academies (*shu-yüan*) and scholarly societies (*she*), which were common in Ming times and occasionally, especially in the late years of the dynasty, were tinged with political purpose.[44] Such associations were principally intended to provide literary and philosophical edification for the membership, however, and governmental officials regularly fostered their development by making financial contributions and by participating in their activities. When they became centers of political agitation, then academies and societies were vulnerable to charges of treasonable partisanship, and the government suppressed them. Several times during the Ming dynasty, all organizations of these types were outlawed.

Despite not having any large-scale formal organization, the gentry was a powerful force in Ming life. On the whole, it was a conservative force. It was interested in maintaining the agrarian values with which its economic status was associated and upon which peasant acquiescence in its demands was based. It was interested in maintaining social stability and public order, essential both to its prestige and its property rights. It therefore willingly cooperated with the government, for its class interests tended to coincide with the political interests of the government. The Ming government, in its turn, refrained from introducing policies that might upset the local dominance of the gentry. Whereas in previous dynasties there had been repeated attempts to undermine the gentry by land redistribution, limitations on landownership, and the like, and whereas the Ming government did actively curb mercantile and industrial prosperity by instituting its own monopolies and by other repressive policies, there seems to have been no governmental inclination in Ming times to interfere with the status quo in the villages. Only the worst extremes of gentry exploitation were dealt with by the government, to alleviate dangerous peasant discontent or to safeguard its own revenues.

INTRA-GOVERNMENTAL RELATIONS

Where power resided in China's imperial state system has been the subject of some dispute. Such was the social eminence of the gentry that it has been suggested imperial China ought to be considered a "gentry society" — one in which economic interests of the landlord class were the basic determinants of governmental policy, and emperors were captives of gentry cliques.[45] To this view is opposed the contention that the regime was instead a genuine despotism, absolutist and autocratic, in which the ruler-controlled state apparatus was stronger than any other societal element and in the last analysis functioned always in the ruler's interest.[46]

A useful distinction might be made here between practice, law, and theory — or, perhaps most precisely, between the ways in which state power was actually exercised, the procedural legitimation of these ways, and their ideological legitimation. The gentry — or some other element in society — might dominate the system in theory, but unless there were available procedural or legal techniques by which it might implement its theoretical predominance in the everyday routine of government, it could hardly be said to have practical control of the system. On the other hand, the system could have been a despotism in law and in practice without being one in theory, if ideological controls exercised by the gentry or other groups were ineffective; and it could have been a despotism in theory and in law without being one in practice, if rulers were not personally inclined to behave despotically. But it could not have been a despotism in practice without being one in law.

There can be no question that in Ming times government was remarkably despotic both in law and in practice. The Ming emperor in his own person was, in a procedural sense, the ultimate source of all state power. Power was exercised at different societal levels by different persons and groups — principally by the various hierarchies of governmental personnel, and on the lowest level, to large extent, by gentry families. But these power-wielders did not hold power in their own right. They merely had access to the emperor's power, either through delegation from him or through tolerated and unpunished usurpation from him or his delegates. Others might bend the emperor to their will, in various direct and indirect ways. Or the emperor might deliberately abandon the exercise of particular powers to others as a matter of personal convenience. But the power was always his, and he was always procedurally free to wield it in the most despotic manner at any given moment, if only he chose to do so. As the foregoing discussion has intimated, there was no independent authority — no church, no aristocracy, no popular assembly — that could lawfully resist him or call him to account.[47]

Politics in Ming China, therefore, was in no sense a competition for supreme power among independent socioeconomic or other societal forces. All other elements in society being formally or procedurally subordinate to the government, politics was a maneuvering for influence within the governmental apparatus itself, and a tenuous hold on the emperor's favor was the only spoil that could legitimately be won.

Total Supremacy of the Emperor

Moreover, the Ming emperors characteristically chose to exercise their powers in a despotic manner. T'ai-tsu (1368–98) was a strong-willed military leader and dictator who in his last years became almost insanely jealous of his imperial prerogatives. He ruthlessly punished Chinese of all classes even for writing words that might be considered punning slurs, intentional or not, on his peasant origins and his early career as Buddhist monk and rebel chief.[48] By the end of his reign he had exterminated many of the powerful men who had helped him establish the dynasty, together with thousands of their relatives and friends. Ch'eng-tsu (1402–24), after taking the throne from his nephew by insurrection, put to death all who might have challenged his usurpation. Ying-tsung (1435–49, 1457–64), Hsien-tsung (1464–87), Wu-tsung (1505–21), Shen-tsung (1572–1620), Hsi-tsung (1620–27), and Ssu-tsung (1627–44) all contemptuously shunned normal administrative processes at times in favor of terroristic rule by eunuch agents. None hesitated to humiliate and punish their governmental servitors dozens or even hundreds at a time. Only two emperors, Hsüan-tsung (1425–35) and Hsiao-tsung (1487–1505), made noteworthy reputations as humane and restrained rulers.

All personnel groups responded to the imperial tyranny by practicing the most abject servility. All state documents were couched in excessively servile phrases, consistently attributing to the emperor — the "ruler-father" — all wisdom, goodness, and other esteemed qualities. However pointed the criticism, it was always sheathed in implications that the emperor, though wise and good, had been misled and deceived by unscrupulous attendants or advisers. However degenerate the emperor, he was always pictured as a paragon of virtue whose gracious benefits no citizen could ever wholly requite. The cumulative effect of all this servility was that, by the late Ming years, officials who were tyrannically sentenced to death for giving offense to the emperor faced the end in the apparently sincere conviction that they had been guilty of the grossest violations of basic human obligations.[49]

The supremacy of the throne was maintained by a variety of techniques. For one thing, the very vastness of the palace within which the emperor and his household attendants were cloistered and the complex ceremonial ritual that enshrouded all the emperor's public appearances invested the throne with a kind of charismatic aura. But the throne was also exalted by procedural arrangements that made all governmental groups necessarily subservient to it.

Imperial clansmen at the beginning of the dynasty were permitted to share in some of the throne's prerogatives. Each prince was given joint control with the emperor over military forces in the region of his official residence. This arrangement made possible the princely insurrection of 1402 that won the throne for Ch'eng-tsu from his nephew. Then the arrangement was promptly altered. Thenceforth, princes exercised no military controls except over small forces serving as personal bodyguards.[50] They were not allowed to interfere in governmental processes of any sort, military, civil, or judicial. The affairs of each prince were managed by a staff of civil service officials assigned by and accountable to the central government. The princes and other clansmen were not allowed to leave their designated provincial residences except with imperial approval, and they married only with imperial approval. Apparently in an effort to forestall powerful combinations among clansmen based on marriage alliances, they were forbidden to marry women of imperial descent.[51] In addition to the salaries paid them by the court, the clansmen were often granted so-called estates, vast tracts of confiscated land and its peasant residents. But the clansman's rights in his estate were proprietary rather than magisterial. Furthermore, the revenue he received from the land was fixed by imperial order, and in time even the collection of rents within the estate was transferred from his control into the hands of line officials of the provincial administrative agencies.[52] Ming princes rose in rebellion twice after Ch'eng-tsu's time, once in 1425 and once in 1519,[53] but neither rebellion was a serious threat to the throne. The privileged status of the clansmen could be exploited socially and economically, but it offered no access to political power; for it was totally dependent on imperial favor.

Imperial in-laws posed an even less dangerous threat to the Ming throne. In earlier dynasties the relatives of empresses and other imperial consorts had frequently gained access to political power and had occasionally even usurped the throne. Historians consider that one of the great achievements of the Ming dynasty was prevention of this type of disruption.[54] The Ming emperors were consciously aware of the political leverage accessible to favored palace women, and they prevented corruption by two techniques. On one hand, they rigorously forbade any effort by palace women to influence governmental activities and made the prohibition effective by keeping their women closely secluded in the palace. So tight was this seclusion that physicians were not even permitted to enter to treat palace women who had fallen ill. On the other hand, emperors did not take into their service any women from already distinguished families. With the single exception of one of Ch'eng-tsu's wives, the daughter of a great general who had been instrumental in the establishment of the dynasty, emperors took their empresses and other principal consorts from families of the common population or from the families of at best relatively low-ranking and insignificant officials, normally of the military service.[55] It was not possible, therefore, for an influential personage in one of the governmental hierarchies to gain dangerous access to imperial power through a marriage alliance with the throne. The arrangement also tended to keep palace women submissive, since they had no relatives outside with independently prestigeful status.

Imperial in-laws were, of course, normally appointed to relatively high-ranking status in the military service or even to the nobility, but only in consequence of the favor in which the palace women were held. Some of them did subsequently enhance their status and prestige by their own service to the throne, and a few eventually exercised some measure of political power; but their status was nevertheless derivative in its essence, and they enjoyed it only at the pleasure of the emperor. They had no independent sources of support in the government or in the population at large.

Other members of the nobility — those who attained their status through their own military exploits — were equally impotent vis-a-vis the throne. Some were favored enough to marry their sons to imperial princesses, and many enjoyed considerable public esteem. But warlordism was avoided by several procedural or organizational arrangements. For one thing, the military establishment came to be so decentralized under five coordinate Chief Military Commissions that no one general could exercise administrative control over more than a fraction of the total forces. Another factor was the Ming system of rotating troops from garrisons into tactical units and back again into garrisons and of assigning tactical commanders arbitrarily from a general pool of nobles and other high-ranking military officers. This meant that garrison officers controlled their troops only in garrison, and combat officers had no long-established personal relationships with the large bodies of troops assigned to them for temporary tactical purposes. It was not procedurally possible, therefore, for a general to accumulate a personal following of numerous combat troops loyal primarily to himself. Moreover, any insurrectionary inclinations that might have existed among the military nobles and officers were frustrated by the

Ming practice of giving responsibility for large-scale coordination of tactical forces only to Supreme Commanders who were career civil-service bureaucrats rather than military officers. The heavy pressures of the late Ming years, which among other things forced the widespread use of mercenaries, necessarily weakened these controls over the military leaders. Nevertheless, the Ming dynasty was never seriously troubled by insurrections led by eminent generals.

Limited Influence of the Civil Service

Officials of the civil service enjoyed somewhat greater independence of status. The powers they wielded in government were legitimated only in part by incumbency as delegates of the emperor. They were also legitimated in some measure by expertize — that is, by competence demonstrated in the public, competitive examinations for entrance into the service.[56] The influence of the civil service was further enhanced by procedural arrangements — exclusion of imperial clansmen and other nobles from offices in the civil administration, subordination of military officers in the field to civil-service Supreme Commanders, subordination of the five Chief Military Commissions to the civil-service Ministry of War in the sphere of strategic planning, and so on. These arrangements tended to give the civil officials a virtual monopoly of all key administrative positions. In prestige, consequently, the civil service over-towered all other personnel groups in the government, with the exception of the imperial family itself. One European visitor to Ming China described this literati dominance:

Another remarkable fact and quite worthy of note as marking a difference from the West, is that the entire kingdom is administered by the Order of the Learned, commonly known as The Philosophers. The responsibility for orderly management of the entire realm is wholly and completely committed to their charge and care. The army, both officers and soldiers, hold them in high respect and show them the promptest obedience and deference, and not infrequently the military are disciplined by them as a schoolboy might be punished by his master. Policies of war are formulated and military questions are decided by The Philosophers only, and their advice and counsel has more weight with the King than that of the military leaders. In fact very few of these, and only on rare occasions, are admitted to war consultations. Hence it follows that those who aspire to be cultured frown upon war and would prefer the lowest rank in the philosophical order to the highest in the military, realizing that the Philosophers far excel military leaders in the good will and the respect of the people and in opportunities of acquiring wealth.[57]

The civil service was also to some extent self-regulating. The entrance examinations were conducted by the Ministry of Rites, and the examiners were themselves high-ranking civil bureaucrats. Promotions and assignments within the service were managed by the Ministry of Personnel, in accordance with elaborately detailed regulations. Appointments to the highest positions were made personally by the emperor, but only by selection from slates of nominees who had been certified as to eligibility on the basis of rank and merit ratings by the Ministry of Personnel and had been nominated by officials of the central government in assembly. I know of no instance, at least after the early formative years of the dynasty, when an emperor arbitrarily promoted a low-ranking official into an important position.

Civil bureaucrats also had a significant role in the formulation of state policy. It was repeatedly proclaimed that no important policy decision would be made without recourse to a court deliberation.[58] This was a formal assembly of important officials charged with considering a given problem and voting for a solution in writing. Composition of the assemblies varied somewhat, according to the kinds of problems being considered, but a standard core was the "nine chief ministers" — the heads of the six Ministries, the Censorate, the Office of Transmission, and the Grand Court of Revision. Each participant seems to have had an equal vote, and unanimity was hoped for. In the late Ming custom a unanimous decision of the assembly was considered binding on the emperor.

Once policy was established, the line agencies of the civil administration carried on routine implementation without being required constantly to seek imperial authorization. At the lower levels of administration, particularly, officials inevitably took many actions with important policy implicaions entirely on their own initiative.

But emperors did not by any means abandon overall administrative authority to their civil officials. It was only custom and their own declared intentions that called upon the rulers to consult with their officials on important matters. There was no procedural hindrance to the arbitrary exercise of their total powers. When policy decisions were to be made, emperors had full right to make them entirely on their own authority, and they often did so. Moreover, they could challenge, reverse, or in any way modify administrative decisions made by anyone in the government. Officials were therefore constantly fearful of being charged with usurpation of authority or of being held to account for decisions that had unpleasing repercussions, and it was their habit servilely to seek specific authorization from the throne for all but the most routine actions. In one ten-day period late in T'ai-tsu's reign, 1,660 memorials dealing with 3,391 separate matters are reported to have been presented for imperial decision.[59]

Of far greater significance in the relationship of the civil officials with the throne was the personal humiliation that they repeatedly suffered. On any pretext at any time officials could be punished in any way ordered by the emperor — by being put to death, being imprisoned and tortured, being exiled to serve as common soldiers at the frontier, being demoted or fined, or being "removed from the register" and thus deprived of status and privileges as state-recognized literati. On one occasion, one-hundred seven officials of the central government were even sentenced to kneel outside the palace gate for five successive days.[60] What was most humiliating of all was that officials could be seized in open-court assembly, stripped naked, and flogged with bamboo poles, sometimes to death.[61] In short, the long-prevalent Western view that the persons of Chinese civil officials were inviolate is simply unfounded in fact, so far as the Ming period is concerned.

Such being their dependence on the whims of the

emperors, it is no wonder that Ming officials cultivated a servile manner. "Instead of recognizing that they are colleagues of the emperor, sharing power with him in order that they may together with him serve the interests of the people," one seventeenth-century Chinese complained, "their only thought is to please him and, like courtesans, attempt to anticipate his every desire. They accept the fact that they, like all else in the land, are the Prince's property, to be disposed of as he pleases."[62] Thus, while they probably enjoyed greater prestige and exercised greater influence vis-a-vis other personnel groups in the government than had their civil service predecessors in prior dynasties, civil officials of the Ming period enjoyed very little prestige vis-a-vis the throne, and they wielded no certain procedural or legal checks on imperial despotism.

One factor that contributed to the impotence of Ming officials before the throne was a lack of cohesion within the civil service as a whole. The literati could not present a disciplined united front against imperial despotism. Instead, their potential for concerted action was constantly thwarted by cleavages of interest among themselves; for the service was honeycombed with partisan cells created by informal personal relationships. Officials who had passed the same doctoral examination, for example, considered themselves life-long comrades who owed political loyalty to one another, and all were bound as disciples into career-long, client-like political subservience to their old examiners. Similar bonds of political clientage persisted between sometime superiors and inferiors in governmental agencies. Thus the adherents of one powerful minister intrigued against those of another, or officials from one region intrigued against those of another region, or officials of one agency against those of others, or literati associated with one philosophical movement against those associated with another, and so on. Since partisan wrangling could only be resolved by one clique's winning imperial favor and ousting its opponents from positions of influence, these struggles served merely to put the whole service increasingly in the despotic control of the throne.[63]

The Special Role of Censorial Surveillance

The disunity that hampered the civil service in its relations with other components of the government derived in part from the nature and activities of the censorial agencies.[64]

Officials of the Censorate, the Offices of Scrutiny, and to a somewhat lesser extent the Provincial Surveillance Offices were specially-licensed critics of the government. Though they were themselves members of the civil service, it was their privilege and duty to stand apart from the line administrative agencies of all sorts and to submit all governmental activities to intense surveillance. They could memorialize on any subject, and their memorials went directly to the throne. They were protected from many potential reprisals by a variety of sophisticated procedural safeguards, and their prestige was bulwarked by a long tradition of censorial audacity.

Because these officials were expected and even exhorted to remonstrate with the emperor about his aberrations, the censorial apparatus had always served as an instrument with which the bureaucracy could sometimes restrain a tyrannical or foolish emperor. By Ming times censors had come to be known popularly as "guardians of *feng* and *hsien*." *Feng* means customs or mores. *Hsien* means fundamental laws or polity; it occurs in the modern Chinese term for the concept "constitution." The censors thus were recognized to be the special defenders of the traditional way of life and the traditional way of government, and many a Ming emperor had to abandon unpopular policies when confronted by the vigorous disapproval of censors representing themselves as spokesmen of the general will. But censorial effectiveness in this regard was reduced somewhat by the censors' hesitance to presume too much upon their relative freedom to remonstrate. The fact was that they had no legal guarantee of tenure and no legal immunity of person; they could be dismissed or punished instantaneously at the whim of the emperor. With few exceptions, they found it prudent to couch their memorials in the same flattering terms as those used by other officials.

On the whole, censorial officials were much more effective and influential in impeaching their fellow bureaucrats, to such a degree that many critics of the Chinese tradition consider the censorial apparatus to have been essentially an instrument with which despotic emperors kept their officials in a state of fearful submission. It was indeed in the power of censors to harass wayward colleagues mercilessly. Their impeachments did not bring automatic convictions and punishments; it was the emperor's decision to act or not to act upon an impeachment. But when a trial was called for it was ordinarily up to the accused to prove himself innocent of the charges, and a particularly convincing accusation could provoke an emperor to punish the accused forthwith, without any trial or hearing. Censorial officials therefore were widely respected.

Inevitably, censors took very active parts in the partisan struggles that repeatedly wracked the Ming officialdom, for a basic tactic of every partisan clique was to win the support of a censorial spokesman. Censors were, to be sure, threatened with severe disciplinary action for abusing their privileged status for irresponsible partisan purposes. But by the latter decades of the Ming period emperors were commonly subjected to such a barrage of conflicting accusations by viciously partisan censors that they found it easiest just to take no note of them at all. This ironically made the censorial accusation a still more effective partisan weapon, for at the same time it had become a matter of honor for many officials, when attacked, to withdraw from service pending exoneration. To rid the government of an enemy, one often needed only to arrange an impeachment, valid or not.

Too often in the late Ming years, consequently, the censorial system served neither as an instrument of bureaucratic control over the monarch nor as an instrument of monarchical control over the bureaucracy, but as a lash with which a sadly fragmented officialdom indulged in paralyzing self-flagellation.

Inner Court Dominance Over the Outer Court

The lack of cohesion within the civil service was related, also, to a tension in the Ming governmental structure between two groups called the "inner court" and the "outer court."[65] "Inner court" was a general term used informally with reference to persons whose functions were intimately connected with the imperial family: palace women, eunuch attendants, and also a group of civil service officials, associated for the most part with the Hanlin Academy, who served as readers-in-waiting, lecturers-in-waiting, proclamation drafters, and tutors of the imperial offspring. "Outer court" was a general term designating the civil service officials of the various agencies of the central government.

In the early years of the dynasty, the outer court, and through it the whole empire-wide administrative apparatus, was integrated rather effectively under the legitimate leadership of the Secretariat, and the Chief Councilors of the Secretariat had strong executive powers, sanctioned primarily by long tradition under prior dynasties. Thus the Secretariat constituted a significant potential check on the absolutism of the emperor. It was precisely for that reason that it was abolished in 1380, and all executive authority was concentrated in imperial hands. T'ai-tsu, moreover, left a warning for his descendants never to permit re-establishment of the Secretariat, and he prescribed the death penalty for anyone who might advocate doing so. This left the outer court leaderless. Chinese critics of the governmental tradition have long recognized that the lack of such leadership — the lack of a prime ministership — was a source of grave political weakness and, possibly, a cause of the eventual collapse of the Ming dynasty.[66]

The beheading of the outer court through abolition

of the Secretariat greatly increased the administrative chores of the emperor, and emperors before long began delegating some of their paperwork to the Grand Secretaries, officially members of the Hanlin Academy, who served the throne as literary consultants and editors. It was obviously T'ai-tsu's intention that these learned gentlemen should be no more than private secretaries. But later emperors, after the fashion of overburdened executives, found it convenient to delegate more and more responsibility to their secretaries, with the result that this group came to serve as a buffer between the emperor and the outer court, with the unofficial designation Grand Secretariat. All incoming documents came to be scrutinized first by the Grand Secretaries, who proposed decisions by drafting rescripts and attaching them to the original documents. When the documents were at last seen by the emperor, he was thus called upon for serious thought only in those cases where the decisions proposed by the Grand Secretaries did not appeal to him. The way was open, consequently, for a senior Grand Secretary to attain to almost the same level of authority as that enjoyed formerly by a prime minister. The Grand Secretariat even came to be referred to commonly as "the administration."

The Grand Secretariat, however, developed, as we would say, entirely outside the constitution. It was never regularized, never officially institutionalized, never recognized openly as an executive organ ranking above the six Ministries. "On paper," as it were, there was no such thing as a Grand Secretariat; there were only individual Grand Secretaries, still officially members of the

Hanlin Academy, ranking far down the civil service scale, well below the senior officials of all the administrative agencies of the central government. This obvious disadvantage was overcome to some extent by a practice of giving Grand Secretaries concurrent nominal ranks as Vice-Ministers or Ministers in the various Ministries; their double ranks then enabled them to take precedence at court assemblies over the functioning heads of the Ministries. But the manager's assistants, so to speak, never became assistant managers. The Grand Secretaries had no formal executive powers. Moreover, despite their nominal concurrent appointments in the Ministries, their preliminary careers in the Hanlin Academy stamped them forever as being essentially members of the inner court. Therefore, although some Grand Secretaries did become strong and influential, officials of the outer court considered them to be personal agents of the emperor and did not accept them as their own spokesmen. Since the Grand Secretaries had no procedural method of giving legitimate disciplinary leadership to the civil service, they became merely new focal points of partisan wrangling.

Palace eunuchs had an even more notable role in the friction between the outer court and the inner court and in intra-governmental strife in general. Some earlier dynasties had fallen partly because of their failure to restrict eunuch access to political power, and the Ming rulers were well aware of this. But they failed to prevent the most notorious examples of eunuch abuses in all Chinese history.[67]

T'ai-tsu felt just as strongly about the dangers of

eunuch influence as he did about the danger of competition from the prime ministership. He maintained only a small force of eunuchs, believed in keeping them illiterate, and forbade on pain of death their interference in governmental affairs. But neither he nor any of his successors seriously heeded the lessons of the past. Ch'engtsu began the extensive employment of eunuchs for special assignments outside the palace, and thereafter they were increasingly used as special investigators, tax collectors, supervisors of foreign trade, directors of state-operated manufactories, and even as military commanders. Eunuchs finally became a dominant factor in Ming political history. Four famous eunuch dictators arose in succession: Wang Chen in the 1440's, Wang Chih in the 1470's, Liu Chin in the early 1500's, and finally the most notorious of all, Wei Chung-hsien, in the 1620's. Under such eunuchs as these, regular administration was totally disrupted.

Ming emperors relied on eunuchs principally for the same reason that English kings of the fourteenth century relied upon celibate clerics to manage their household agencies such as the exchequer and the chancery: that is, their loyalty to the throne was not diluted with family concerns to the same extent as was that of officials who must provide for their heirs.[68] Moreover, since eunuchs necessarily came from the lowest classes in society and were objects of revulsion to persons of respectable backgrounds, they had little hope of attaining status or esteem except through faithful and pleasing service to their imperial master. They were not affected by public opinion, and they need never be influenced by the moralistic considerations that colored the literati's every act. They had nothing whatsover to gain by opposing the emperor's whims and everything to gain by acquiescing in them. Their subservience, consequently, was the most total of all, and emperors seem to have considered them to be singularly trustworthy.

Since the emperor relied on eunuchs for the satisfaction of personal, everyday wants, they had no difficulty in gaining access to him. And, since they were the only males who were permitted to have informal daily contact with him, they had unequaled opportunities to become his confidants. Young or weak emperors, therefore, easily fell under the influence of strong-willed eunuchs, and dilatory emperors gladly utilized vigorous and clever eunuchs to do much of their work for them. At times eunuchs became go-betweens essential to the maintenance of even remote contact between the emperor and the officialdom. Shen-tsung (1572–1620), an extreme case, allowed twenty-five years to pass without once having audience with his capital officials and allowed a decade to pass without even consulting in person with a Grand Secretary. At such times, imperial decisions were transmitted to the Grand Secretariat on papers carried by eunuchs shuttling in and out of the remote recesses of the palace, and sometimes they were even transmitted orally. Improper eunuch influence on state affairs was almost unavoidable.

The officialdom seems to have been helpless in this situation. Even Grand Secretaries had no choice but to connive with influential eunuchs so as to maintain essential governmental activities, which depended heavily on obtaining prompt decisions or confirmations of decisions from the throne. And partisan-minded officials involved in struggles between cliques further weakened the integrity of the civil service by currying favor with influential eunuchs through bribery and flattery. As I have had occasion to suggest elsewhere,[69] the organizational structure and the procedural arrangements of the Ming government, except in the reigns of diligent and conscientious emperors, did not permit political success to any but the unprincipled.

The Influence of Lesser Functionaries

One other aspect of intra-governmental relations should also be mentioned: the influence that the Ming system permitted lesser functionaries to exercise.[70]

Lesser functionaries were, generally speaking, the office clerks who assisted the civil service officials in the administrative routine. They outnumbered the officials by a ratio of at least four to one. Locally recruited at all levels and not subject to regular civil service regulations, they were the only staff members of every governmental agency who had continuing status. They characteristically spent their whole careers in the same office, and often they passed their positions on to their sons. As executive-like officials came and went on their limited-tenure assignments, the continuity and efficiency of governmental operations depended upon the clerks' mastery of details. They were, of course, dependent in some degree upon the approval of their superiors; but the officials were perhaps more dependent on their know-how. Careers could be ruined by inept clerical work.

An official newly assigned to a given agency was totally unfamiliar with the technical details of its operations. His preparations for a civil service career had been general and largely literary. He therefore had to learn the details of his work on the job, and he had to learn them from his clerks. The traditions of the office and the entrenched interests of the clerks inevitably shaped his conception of what he was expected to do. As often as not, he was transferred away to a new post before he had become wholly familiar with the old.

The opportunities for undue influence on the part of clerical functionaries were undoubtedly greatest in the county governmental establishments. Most county magistrates seem to have been serving in their first civil service assignments, fresh from their successes in the doctoral examinations. They therefore had no prior experience of clerical wiles and misrepresentations. Moreover, they were total strangers to the areas in which they found themselves; for no Ming civil servant was allowed to accept a local-level assignment in his home province. The intent of this "law of avoidance" was to prevent nepotistic influences on magistrates, but its effect was to enhance the magistrate's dependence on his clerks. He did not know the peculiarities of local customs or the pitfalls of local politics. Were it not for the guidance of his clerks, he could easily blunder into awkward relationships or embarrassing commitments. At worst, so great is the diversity of dialects in some areas of China, he might not even be able to communicate directly with the people of his jurisdiction. The clerks consequently were in a position to control, in their own interests, the impact of government on local communities. The only effective counterweight to their influence was that of the local gentry families.

We do not have data that permit close analysis of what lesser functionaries actually did or of the social composition of the clerical staff in any given governmental agency of Ming times. But it would probably be unrealistic to think that the gentry families allowed positions of such potential influence to remain outside their control. In all probability, the lesser functionaries in all county governmental establishments, at least, were representatives, in some degree, of the local gentry families and wielded their influence in such a way as to augment gentry dominance over local affairs.

THE NATURE OF GOVERNMENTAL ACTIVITY

The despotism in law and in practice that characterized the Ming governmental system was tempered by ideological considerations. The regime was a despotism even in theory, but it was expected to be a benevolent despotism; and this expectation influenced all aspects of governmental activity.

The Supremacy of Confucianism

The expectation was rooted in the Confucian system of philosophy, as expounded originally by such ancient thinkers as Confucius and Mencius, as related systematically to government by Tung Chung-shu in the second century B.C., as revised by various Neo-Confucian thinkers of the eleventh and twelfth centuries A.D., and as perpetuated by all men of education from generation to generation in Ming times. Through its successive transformations, the philosophy had become so inextricably involved with the Chinese way of life in its totality that imperial China is commonly designated a Confucian society or a Confucian state.

The Ming state was Confucian in the sense that it espoused Confucianism as its official ideology. Ming rulers sanctified their authority by appealing to Confucian dogma about human society and the larger universe, and they entrusted administration largely to civil service bureaucrats selected in examinations which principally tested their mastery of the Confucian texts and principles.

When Confucianism was first adopted as the orthodox state ideology a millenium and a half before the Ming era, rulers were probably drawn to it in part because it seemed to serve their own despotic interests. But it would be misleading to suggest that in Ming times Confucianism was merely an ideological tool utilized by rulers to achieve optimum satisfaction of their despotic wants. For Ming rulers were themselves tools of the philosophical system they espoused, to such an extent that they had no real choice but to espouse it and to govern in general accord with its principles. They could not possibly have done otherwise. Therefore, although it is true that ideological controls were not sufficiently implemented in law to prevent a despotic emperor from achieving a particular goal, the ideology largely determined what his goals were.

This was so because Confucianism dominated the realm of learning and the realm of governmental discourse. Emperors-to-be were tutored from infancy in Confucian materials by Hanlin Academy officials of distinguished scholarly reputations, and their continuing education after taking the throne was in the hands of Hanlin readers-in-waiting and expositors-in-waiting. Thus in learning of the world he lived in and of its history — or, for that matter, in merely becoming literate — the emperor was subjected to powerful Confucian influences. Moreover, governmental problems were discussed only in Confucian terminology, and governmental documents were composed only in the literary styles of which Confucian literati were masters. There was no other manner in which to transact public affairs. Merely by participating in governmental discourse day after day, therefore, the emperor unavoidably accepted basic Confucian assumptions.

The supremacy of Confucianism had important implications for the relationship between civil servants and the throne. For Confucianism was the particular profession of the literati — or the gentry, if it is assumed that the two groups were identical. I have already noted that the political powers of the literati were legitimated by expertize as well as by incumbency. I mean by this that the literati, being certified by the state as having mastered the principles of Confucianism, were popularly considered to be exemplars of wisdom, morality, and public-spiritedness. They were honored by their communities, they were sought after as educators of the new generation, and their judgments on public and private affairs were given great weight. They were the natural leaders of society.

The Confucian bureaucrat was not, in his own view, a professional bureaucrat. His profession was Confucian learning — or, in another sense, conserving the values of traditional Chinese civilization. He was all at once a poet, painter, essayist, calligrapher, philosopher, moralist, and arbiter of good taste. That his competence qualified him for bureaucratic status was almost coincidental. This does not mean that he disdained government service, or that he sought government service only for material reward. Because government is an essential aspect of society in the Confucian scheme of things, he necessarily viewed participation in government as an important element of Confucian morality and a natural fulfillment of his Confucian profession. But, if he were conscientious, he did not hesitate to abandon his bureaucratic career at any time when its continuation involved a violation of the Confucian code of ethics.

Human relationships were the most important thing in the Confucian code. A Confucian must be filial to his parents, and he must be loyal to the emperor. In the prevalent Neo-Confucianism of Ming times, it is quite clear that loyalty to the emperor ranked more highly in the scale of obligations than had been the case in prior times. Nevertheless, it remained true that filial piety took precedence over loyalty to the emperor, should these conflict. Above all, adherence to the Confucian system itself was an obligation of the first priority, taking theoretical precedence over all else. It would have been theoretically unjustifiable for a Confucian to appeal to the "reason of state" — the Machiavellian doctrine that survival of the political order transcends other requirements. No one could really conceive that the system might change, even with a change of dynasty; for the political order was thought to be an integral part of the natural order. Thus, for example, even the highest-ranking minister of state expected to observe mourning for a dead parent by retiring from office for twenty-seven months, no matter what the exigencies of the time.

This conditional loyalty must have been a source of much annoyance to the Ming emperors, since they often found their more autocratic inclinations frustrated in part, if not wholly, by the remonstrances, the slow-down tactics, and the occasional outright defiance of moralistic Confucian ministers. But the Ming rulers tolerated bureaucratic obstruction and half-hearted loyalty because they still needed the Confucian bureaucracy.

This was certainly not because the Confucian literati monopolized any special managerial skills. In a sense, moralistic Confucian indoctrination stifled administrative efficiency. One would almost suppose that the merchant community might well have provided more effective fiscal administrators, and that Buddhist and Taoist monks might have made more pliant secretaries. The Mongols, during their relatively short rule in China, used many non-Confucians and even non-Chinese in their administration; and the Ming emperors, as has already been indicated, relied heavily on eunuchs, who were practically never indoctrinated Confucians. But Confucian bureaucrats had to be relied on over the long run. I think this is partly because Confucian education tended to produce men who, more than others who were at hand, could be counted on to have some measure of genuine public-spiritedness and personal integrity — virtues that any governmental executive would hope to find in his subordinates. But, even more than this, I suspect the Confucian bureaucrat was indispensable to rulers because the Chinese people at large would not contentedly be governed by others. Such was the charismatic prestige of Confucian learning.

Ideological considerations, then, might be said to have controlled Ming despotism *in general,* even though organizational and procedural arrangements did not permit them to control despotism *in particulars*. In the very last analysis, government operated in the interests, not of the ruler, but of the Confucian system and thus of the literati or gentry, its principal advocates.

Some Fundamental Ideological Considerations

The foundation of all Confucian political theory is a religious belief in Heaven. The Confucian Heaven is the supreme summation of natural forces: the ultimate source of all creation and the ultimate arbiter of the destinies of all things. Though impersonal, it is wilful; and it wills that all things fulfill their proper roles in nature. It thus wills that men be good — that they enjoy material, social, intellectual, and spiritual well-being. Moreover, Heaven has its ways of chastening those who violate its will.

The Chinese emperor was considered to be the earthly legate of Heaven. Though popularly called the Son of Heaven, he was in no sense divine; but he was the semi-theocratic intermediary in all things between Heaven and the masses of mankind. His authority was legitimated by the trust that Heaven reposed in him; and he was in turn responsible to Heaven for the goodness and well-being of mankind. He was also responsible to the spirits of his dynastic forebears, who had a continuing interest in the affairs of their family and who in some fashion wielded influence in Heaven. Unusual astronomical phenomena were thought to be warnings from Heaven, and emperors were expected to respond to them with ritual acts of contrite appeasement and with concrete reforms. Natural calamities — floods, droughts, plagues of locusts, and so on — were manifestations of Heaven's active displeasure; and a successful rebellion was prima facie evidence that Heaven, despairing of its legate, had transferred its mandate to someone else. The emperor therefore ruled by a form of popular consent rather than by divine right in the traditional Western sense.

Since the emperor as legate of Heaven was responsible for the total well-being of mankind, government was thoroughly paternalistic. The state was a macrocosmic family in which the emperor was father and mother of the people, and the civil service officials who were his delegates in the line administrative agencies were popularly known as father-and-mother officials.

Governmental Services and Obligations

These ideological considerations determined the nature of governmental activities. At least in Ming China, they provided for a welfare state of all-encompassing scope.[71]

Performance of proper rituals was one of the most notable obligations of the government; for only by a ritualistic approach to life could the Chinese hope to accord harmoniously with the way of nature. The Ministry of Rites was a highly esteemed agency of the central government, and such important matters as the civil service examinations and the conduct of tributary relations were in its charge. The government sponsored astrological research in an effort to determine the natural rhythm of the universe and to interpret the significance of its disruptions. Government astrologers prepared annual calendars or almanacs that were distributed to all subjects as guides to the proper times for planting, harvesting, and other cyclical activities. The emperor inaugurated the spring season each year with a ritual plowing; he performed elaborate ceremonial sacrifices to Heaven and to Earth upon great altars in the capital; he conducted ritual worship in the ancestral temple of the imperial family. Officials at all levels fulfilled comparable ritual obligations by sacrificing regularly to local spirits of the land and of the crops, to local tutelary spirits of various sorts, and to the spirit of their own patron saint, Confucius. They also prayed for rain and for the recession of floods. All the transactions of everyday governmental business were influenced by ritualistic prescriptions about procedures, staging, and dress. The vast Ming code of administrative procedures, *Ta Ming Hui-tien,* devotes seventy-five of its two hundred twenty-eight chapters to the responsibilities of the Ministry of Rites — more than to any other single branch of government. Anyone who works extensively with Ming documents, consequently, cannot avoid the conclusion that proper government in the Ming view was largely a matter of performing proper rituals.

The government also recognized educational responsibilities. It established an integrated school system extending from local schools at the county level up to the National University at the capital; it subsidized students in state schools; it prescribed operation of a free community school as one of the responsibilities of each community chief in the population at large; it sanctioned and to some extent subsidized privately organized scholarly academies. By adopting Confucianism as the curriculum of the civil service examinations, it standardized the content of education throughout the empire, and it suppressed teachings that were considered heterodox. It stimulated learning by financing the compilation and publication of scholarly works in various fields, by granting valued privileges to successful candidates in the examinations, and by honoring distinguished scholars of the past with official sacrificial ceremonies. Moreover, since the aim of education was primarily moral edification, the government supplemented all these activities with constant pronouncements from the throne that urged the people to emulate the great worthies of antiquity in observing their moral obligations. Violations of filial piety or other breaches of traditional morality, though entirely private matters by modern Western standards, were punishable by the state. Conversely, those who distinguished themselves as paragons of virtue — sons who made great sacrifices for their parents, or widows who remained extraordinarily faithful to their dead husbands, for example — were rewarded by the officialdom, praised by the emperor, and in other ways held up to public esteem. Public morality was an integral element in Heaven's way of the universe, and the Ming state was its guardian.

There was also vigorous state promotion of economic welfare. Maintaining equality of economic opportunity seems to have been one of its aims; for the government established state monopolies and pursued restrictive policies in such a way as to curb private mercantile and industrial exploitation of the general population, and on the other hand it tried to prevent at least the worst forms of gentry-landlord oppression in the agrarian sphere. But these concerns did not exhaust the government's economic interests. Agencies at all levels of provincial government were required to utilize public stores of grain as a check on inflationary price fluctuations, by buying and selling at appropriate times; and the prices of non-agricultural commodities were controlled by local officials. In times of acute distress, government stores of grain were distributed in relief, and tax remissions were granted. Moreover, the government sponsored the building of dykes for flood control, the digging and maintenance of irrigation ditches to facilitate agricultural production, and the operation of roads and waterways for travel and transport. When natural disasters or rebellions devastated large areas, the government undertook to resettle displaced persons and provided them with tools, draft animals, and tax exemptions that would permit them to re-establish themselves. New lands were regularly opened to agricultural use under government auspices. In short, no aspect of Chinese economic life was immune from state interference; and the government assumed responsibility for economic prosperity.

Like all other governments, the Ming government administered justice. There was a law code of 460 articles that was promulgated by T'ai-tsu in 1397, after several revisions of drafts. It was a unitary code consolidating criminal law, civil law, and sumptuary law, but organized into six sections corresponding to the administrative spheres of the six Ministries in the central government. Most precisely, it was a compendium of administrative regulations, condensed and codified; it set forth the obligations of all persons to society and the state, and prescribed punishments for violations. The law was administered by the general civil administration hierarchy, without any separation of judicial from administrative functions except in the upper echelons. Moreover, there was no bar of private legal specialists and no jury system, except that important judicial cases might be entrusted to court deliberations. In the general administration of criminal and civil laws, the local magistrate was himself prosecutor, police investigator, defense counsel, judge, and jury. But there was the possibility of appeal to higher and ever higher administrative echelons, and important cases were subjected to routine review up the administrative ladder. There was no effort to correlate judicial action with the letter of the law; for the law code was considered no more than a general guide to magistrates, insofar as its criminal and civil sections were concerned. Moreover, there was no concept of abstract justice. The duty of the magistrate was to determine the facts of a crime or a dispute and then to render a reasonable, equitable decision based upon the status, the relationships, and the social obligations of the parties, the degree of moral culpability involved in their acts, and the needs of the community or of society at large. Ming justice, in short, was a very relative thing. Its aim was to serve the cause of social stability and general welfare rather than to preserve abstract individual rights.

Self-maintenance was another principal obligation of the state. This had a military aspect and a fiscal aspect. The government maintained a very large military establishment. But, as has been noted already, the military forces were used for aggression only rarely, and even then aggressive attack was considered to be essentially a defensive stratagem. There was no urge for conquest. As a contemporary European observer remarked, "it seems to be quite remarkable when we stop to consider it, that in a kingdom of almost limitless expanse and innumerable population, and abounding in copious supplies of every description, though they have a well-equipped army and navy that could easily conquer the neighboring nations, neither the King nor his people ever think of waging a war of aggression. They are quite content with what they have and are not ambitious of conquest. In this respect they are much different from the people of Europe . . ."[72]

The large governmental establishment naturally required enormous revenues for its support. The principal levy was that on agricultural land, assessed on families according to a complex formula that took account of the quality as well as the quantity of the land owned. In the sixteenth century the levy of corvée labor, based on persons, was consolidated with the land tax into a single, relatively simple assessment based on land, called the Single Whip.[73] Originally, taxes were collected either in natural kind — principally grain — or in government-circulated currency — copper coins and paper money as well. But bulk silver in units of *taels* (Chinese ounces) increasingly became the dominant medium of exchange and, especially after the Single Whip reform, the principal component of governmental revenues. Part of these revenues was retained in the provinces to take care of local needs, and a larger part was forwarded to Peking. A fleet of some two thousand ships was maintained by the government specifically to transport such revenues from South China along the Grand Canal, which connected Peking to Hang-chou south of modern Shanghai. Total revenues and expenditures of the government naturally fluctuated somewhat at all times, but they steadily grew. In one unspecified year of the Wan-li reign (1573–1620), when revenues had largely been converted from grain to silver, the budget of the central government amounted to 4,358,244 *taels* of silver and 2,356,584 bushels of grain.[74] Thereafter taxes were repeatedly increased to meet defense needs in the face of Manchu challenges from the north. By 1635, revenues in silver had increased to more than twelve million *taels*,[75] and military expenditures alone are reported to have grown to twenty million *taels* of silver annually by 1639.[76] Certainly in these last years of the dynasty, but almost equally at all other times, a considerable proportion of the total governmental effort had to be devoted to the assessment, collection, management, and disbursement of these state revenues.

A final major governmental activity in the Ming system was self-regulation. This included the censorial surveillance already referred to. Otherwise, it was a matter of routine personnel management under the Ministry of Personnel. Appointments, reassignments, transfers, promotions, demotions, ranks, honorific titles, retirements, pensions—the handling of all these matters, especially within the civil service, amounted to a substantial governmental activity, and the prestige of personnel management was so great that the Minister of Personnel was understood to take precedence over his counterparts of other Ministries in court ceremonies, although all were equal in rank.

Governmental Sanctions

To enforce its will in these various spheres of activity, the state made use of coercive sanctions. Five kinds of punishments were officially prescribed: (1) from ten to fifty strokes of the bamboo, (2) from sixty to one hundred strokes of the bamboo, (3) from one to three years of temporary banishment — that is, excluding one from residence in his native place — coupled with from sixty to one hundred strokes of the bamboo, (4) permanent banishment — usually to serve as a soldier in the frontier forces — at a distance of from two thousand to three thousand Chinese miles *(li)* from one's native place, coupled with one hundred strokes of the bamboo, and (5) death, either by strangulation or by decapitation.[77] Persons awaiting sentence or execution were detained in prison, and often for very long periods, but imprisonment was not itself considered to be an official punishment. Legal tortures, which magistrates freely used to obtain confessions or to discipline unruly prisoners, included beating with the bamboo and the use of such instruments as finger-presses, fetters, and especially a kind of portable pillory called a cangue. Beating with the bamboo was especially dreaded; for the first blow usually drew blood, and application of more than fifty blows was often fatal.[78]

The threat and use of punishment was unquestionably an effective tool of Ming despotism, and the threat became greater than ever in the latter half of the dynasty, when palace eunuchs combined with troops of the imperial bodyguard, called the Embroidered-Uniform Guard, to operate a terroristic secret service outside the regular judicial channels.[79] Contemporary European observers vividly described the sufferings of Ming prisoners, some on the basis of their own personal experience.[80]

The use of military force was another aspect of governmental coercion. Garrison troops were regularly called upon to quell public disturbances,[81] and even in periods of notable order and peace the Ming annals are full of reports of military actions against bandits and peasant rebels.[82] There was no hesitance at all to rely upon military force if it was needed to preserve the authority of the government.

State reliance upon punishments and military coercion, however, directly violated the principles of Confucianism. It was always recognized, of course, that some coercive measures had to be used in the preservation of social stability, and some ancient competitors of Confucianism, of the school called Legalism, had openly advocated ruthless coercion. But Confucius himself had consistently argued against coercion as a proper state sanction, and Tung Chung-shu had established the orthodox dogma: "A state which relies only upon punishment opposes Heaven."[83] In the Ming system, although it is true that coercion "remained a cornerstone of official policy,"[84] it was generally relied upon only in what the authorities considered the last resort. European visitors to Ming China, on the whole, give a favorable impression of Chinese justice as compared with European. They praised judicial restraint in general and were especially impressed by the hesitance of the officialdom to impose the death sentence.[85] One remarked that "With respect to the punishment of crime, one would say that in general Chinese authorities are rather remiss..."[86] They noted, too, the remarkable Chinese capacity for maintaining order without extensive police surveillance.

Ming Confucians preferred persuasion to coercion. The educational system and the constant exhortations issued from the throne and from the officialdom were thought to be the best guarantees of general welfare. In case of popular uprisings or banditry, emperors commonly sent out officials to persuade the malcontents to submit and reform by reading to them "soothing edicts," in the hope that military action might not have to be resorted to.[87] And emperors constantly justified even their most arbitrary and harsh actions on the ground that persuasion had proved ineffective.

But Confucianism basically relied upon the force of example. Confucius had said, "Govern the people by regulations, keep order among them by chastisements, and they will flee from you, and lose all self-respect. Govern them by moral force, keep order among them by ritual and they will keep their self-respect and come to you of their own accord."[88] And in one of his most famous dicta about government he said, "The essence of the gentleman is that of wind; the essence of small people is that of grass. And when a wind passes over the grass, it cannot choose but bend."[89] It was this belief in the efficacy of moral example that led Ming emperors to do public honor to exemplars of moral virtues among the people, to entrust administration principally to non-specialist literati, and to blame themselves publicly for national misfortunes. For good government was thought to depend, in the last resort, on the charismatic virtues of the ruling class.

THE GENERAL TONE OF GOVERNMENTAL OPERATIONS

All the aspects of government that have so far been discussed — the structural organization, the inter-group relations, the scope of activities, the ideological rationalization, and so on — combine to give Ming government a distinctive style or tone that is readily sensed by every student of Ming documents.

One notable feature of this tone is that there was only moderate stress on administrative efficiency. It is true that the government's organizational structure was quite complex, and its component units were neatly articulated. Moreover, their activities were governed by detailed and voluminous regulations. One observes at every hand the remarkable sophistication of governmental operations. But one notes, too, that in the actual practice of government there was no semblance of machine-like impersonality. Governmental workers were clearly expected to be only moderately observant of prescribed procedures. Bureaucratism was not an ideal.

The Ming bureaucracy, in other words, was not dehumanized. Personal factors always intruded into governmental considerations, and personal morality was the transcendent value. The way to solve problems was not to debate abstractly about policies and stratagems, but to appoint good men to deal with them. And the way to evaluate proposals was to consider the characters of the men who proposed them rather than their own intrinsic merits. Since men were good by moral definition principally, their intentions tended to be more important than the practical results they achieved. As a matter of fact, evidence of good intentions usually led to the assumption that good results had been achieved; and so long as an official's moral character was unchallenged, much could be forgiven him — inefficiency or worse. In general, then, and in accord with the Confucian ideal, Ming government was government by men rather than government by law.

The governmental tone was not only intensely personal; it was intensely conservative. There was a strong sense of historical continuity, rooted in ancestor worship. No emperor could think lightly of departing from the precedents established by his forebears. The policies and pronouncements of the founding emperors, T'ai-tsu and Ch'eng-tsu, were revered by their successors as a kind of dynastic constitution; and the early emperors, for their part, had consciously based their policies and pronouncements on those of great rulers of the past. For Ming emperors and officials alike, history was a manual of statecraft, and they constantly referred to its lessons. Nothing could be done except in accord with historical precedents. Moreover, the sanction of precedent was often invoked in the most narrow and rigid fashion. When the Portuguese first arrived in China, for example, they were denied participation in normal tributary relationships because, although the tributary pattern itself was well established for dealing with non-Chinese peoples, extensive searching of the historical records could produce no precedent for the participation of the Portuguese in particular.

In a very real sense, therefore, Ming government was a trust inherited from the long past. It was not a process of aggressive, forward-looking advancing toward new goals, but a process of conserving what had been bequeathed by the ancestors.

NOTES

[1] For a detailed description of the Ming governmental apparatus, see my article "Governmental Organization of the Ming Dynasty," *Harvard Journal of Asiatic Studies*, XXI (1958), 1–66.

[2] The throne was normally expected to pass from father to eldest son, and it did pass from father to son in ten instances; but it passed twice from eldest brother to younger brother, once from grandfather to grandson, once from cousin to cousin, and once even from nephew to uncle. The longest reign of the dynasty was forty-eight years, the shortest was one month, and the mean was between sixteen and seventeen years. By Chinese reckoning, which counts every calendar year in which one has lived as a year of his age *(sui)*, the average age of all emperors at enthronement was twenty-three and the average age at death was forty-two. Eight of the emperors came to the throne as minors, the youngest at the age of nine. The oldest at enthronement was forty-seven. None lived longer than the founding emperor, who died at the age of seventy-one, and the earliest death of a reigning emperor came at the age of twenty-three. See biographical data on the successive emperors in the Main Annals *(Pen-chi)* sections of *Ming-shih* (the official "Ming History," hereinafter cited as MS; the Po-na ed.).

[3] The following discussion of the imperial clan is based principally on MS, chaps. 100–04 and 121.

[4] Wu Han, *Chu Yüan-chang Chuan* (Shanghai, 1949), pp. 262–63.

[5] See MS, chap. 74, pp. 32*a*–33*b;* chap. 113, pp. 1*a*–2*a*.

[6] Ting I, *Ming-tai T'e-wu Cheng-chih* (Peking, 1950), p. 24.

[7] See MS, chap. 74, pp 24a–32a, chap. 304, *passim;* Ting I, *op. cit., passim.*

[8] Ting I, *op. cit.*, pp. 22–26. Cf. C. Alvarez Semedo, *The History of That Great and Renowned Monarchy of China . . .* , trans. from the Italian "by a person of quality" (London, 1655), p. 116; and Matthew Ricci, *China in the Sixteenth Century: The Journals of Matthew Ricci, 1583–1610,* trans. from the Latin by L. J. Gallagher (New York, 1953), p. 87.

[9] See *Ta Ming Hui-tien* (hereinafter cited as TMHT; *Wan-yu Wen-k'u* ed.), chap. 80 (vol. 141, pp. 1837–38). G. Carter Stent, in his article "Chinese Eunuchs," *Journal of the North China Branch, Royal Asiatic Society,* n.s. XI (1877), 143–84, indicates that in imperial days generally the candidates for eunuch status were castrated within the palace; but I have seen no confirmation of this in Ming materials. C. Alvarez Semedo states, to the contrary, that at intervals "there comes almost infinite of these *Eunuchs* to the Court, who are made such by their parents; either for the profit which they make by it, because they are always bought of them for a price, or else for the advantages they may receive by them, when they come to preferment in the Palace, or for those other conveniences, which are certaine and assured to persons of this condition." He adds, "At every election, there are chosen about 3000 of them; at what time they principally consider in their choice, their age, good shape and behaviour, their speech and gracefull pronunciation, but above all, that they wholly want that, which they pretend to have lost, and that they be completely *castrated;* and moreover, every fourth year they are visited, lesst any thing should grow out againe, which hath not been well taken away." (*Op. cit.*, p. 116). In 1621, when 3,000 new eunuchs were desired for the palace, more than 20,000 candidates were offered, according to *Hsi-tsung Shih-lu* (photolithographic reproduction, 1940), chap. 1, pp. 6a–6b.

[10] Ting I, *op. cit.*, p. 23.

[11] See MS, chap. 76, pp. 1b–2a, chaps. 105–08.

[12] See MS, chap. 72, pp. 6a–11a, also chaps. 69–71. Cf. Hucker, *op. cit.*, pp. 11–17.

[13] Hucker, *op. cit.*, p. 12. Cf. *Hsiao-t'ien Chi-chuan* (Nanking, 1887), chap. 12, pp. 5b–6a.

[14] See *Hsü Wen-hsien T'ung-k'ao* (imperial compilation; Shanghai, 1936), chap. 35.

[15] See TMHT, chap. 7–8. Cf. Hucker, *op. cit.*, pp. 18–19.

[16] See MS, chaps. 76 and 89–92.

[17] *T'ai-tsu Shih-lu* (photolithographic reproduction, 1940), chap. 223, p. 8a; *Hsü Wen-hsien T'ung-k'ao*, chap. 51, p. 3255; Fu Wei-lin, *Ming-shu* (Shanghai, 1928) chap. 72, p. 1454.

[18] Karl A. Wittfogel, *Oriental Despotism: A Comparative Study of Total Power* (New Haven, 1957), pp. 49–50.

[19] See MS, chap. 76, pp. 21a–22a.

[20] See T. C. Lin, "Manchuria in the Ming Empire," *Nankai Social and Economic Quarterly*, VIII (1935), 1–43; T. C. Lin, "Manchurian Trade and Tribute in the Ming Dynasty," *op. cit.*, IX (1936), 855–92; and Y. T. Wang, *Official Relations Between China and Japan, 1368–1549* (Cambridge, Mass., 1953).

[21] Semedo, *op. cit.*, p. 19.

[22] See, for example, Chang T'ien-tse, *Sino-Portuguese Trade from 1514 to 1644* (Leiden, 1934); and Arnold H. Rowbotham, *Missionary and Mandarin: The Jesuits at the Court of China* (Berkeley, 1942).

[23] See Ping-ti Ho, *Studies on the Population of China, 1368–1953* (Cambridge, Mass., 1959), pp. 3–23 and 277. Professor Ho "guesses" that the population had probably reached one-hundred fifty million by 1600. Cf. O. B. van der Sprenkel, "Population Statistics in Ming China," *Bulletin of the School of Oriental and African Studies*, University of London, XV, part 2 (1953), 289–326; and J. K. Fairbank, *The United States and China* (rev. ed.; Cambridge, Mass., 1958), p. 124.

[24] MS, chap. 40, *passim*.

[25] The Ming system of sub-county organization is described in MS, chap. 78; Liang Fang-chung, *The Single-whip Method of Taxation in China* (Cambridge, Mass., 1956); and Huang Wei-k'un, *Chou Han T'ang Sung Ming Ti-fang Chih-tu K'ao* (Shanghai, 1906), pp. 44 ff. Cf van der Sprenkel, *op. cit.*, p. 309; Wu Han, *op. cit.*, pp. 141–44; and Semedo, *op. cit.*, p. 131. K. C. Hsiao, "Rural Control in Nineteenth Century China," *Far Eastern Quarterly*, XII (1952–53), 173–81, is useful for comparison.

[26] Huang Wei-k'un, *op. cit.*, pp. 44–46. Cf. Hui-chen Wang Liu, "An Analysis of Chinese Clan Rules: Confucian Theories in Action," in *Confucianism in Action*, ed. D. S. Nivison and A. F. Wright (Stanford, 1959), pp. 72–73. See K. C. Hsiao, *op. cit.*, p. 176, note 13, for the similar formula utilized in the Ch'ing dynasty.

[27] Huang Wei-k'un, *op. cit.*, pp. 46–47.

[28] K. C. Hsiao, *op. cit.*, p. 178. Cf. Wittfogel, *op. cit.*, pp. 125–26.

[29] Ricci, *op. cit.*, p. 105.

[30] Wu Han, *op. cit.*, especially pp. 125 ff.

[31] See Ku Ying-t'ai, *Ming-shih Chi-shih Pen-mo* (*Wan-yu Wen-k'u* ed.), chap. 70.

[32] See MS, chap. 74, pp. 22*b*–23*b*; chap. 75, pp. 23*b*–24*a*.

[33] Wang Hsiao-t'ung, *Chung-kuo Shang-yeh Shih* (Shanghai, 1936), p. 167.

[34] *Ibid.*, pp. 161 ff.; Wu Chao-ts'ui, *Chung-kuo Shui-chih Shih* (Shanghai, 1937), I, 128, 168–71, 180–82; MS, chap. 81, pp. 15*b*–21*b*. One European observer thought the Ming domestic customs houses operated very fairly and honestly in comparison with those of Europe. Semedo, *op. cit.*, p. 12.

[35] Wang Hsiao-t'ung, *op. cit.*, p. 167.

[36] *Ibid.*, p. 163; Wu Chao-ts'ui, *op. cit.*, I, 172–73.

[37] See MS, chap. 80–81; Wu Chao-ts'un, *op. cit.*, I, 149–60.

[38] Wu Chao-ts'ui, *op. cit.*, I, 150.

[39] *Ibid.*, I, 158; Chang Liang-ts'ai, *Chung-kuo Feng-su Shih* (Shanghai, 1928), p. 161.

[40] For a detailed discussion of gentry oppression, especially in the late Ming years, see Li Wen-chih, *Wan Ming Min-pien* (Shanghai, 1948), pp. 1–14.

[41] *Ibid.*, and Hsieh Kuo-chen, *Ming Ch'ing Chih Chi Tang-she Yün-tung K'ao* (Shanghai, 1934), pp. 257 ff.

[42] Wu Chao-ts'ui, *op. cit.*, I, 171.

[43] See Franz Michael, "State and Society in Nineteenth-century China," *World Politics*, VII, No. 3 (April 1955), 419–33; and Chang Chung-li, *The Chinese Gentry: Studies on Their Role in Nineteenth-Century Chinese Society* (Seattle, 1955). In the absence of detailed analytical studies of the Ming gentry, I cannot

be certain that these interpretations of the nineteenth-century situation are applicable to the earlier period, but the Ming materials I have seen tend to support the notion that gentry status then, as later, was virtually inseparable from governmental service.

44 See Sheng Lang-hsi, *Chung-kuo Shu-yüan Chih-tu* (Shanghai, 1934), chap. 4; Chang Liang-ts'ai, *op. cit.*, pp. 168–69; and Hsieh Kuo-chen, *op. cit*. For studies of the political influence of one Ming academy see my article "The Tung-lin Movement of the Late Ming Period," in *Chinese Thought and Institutions,* ed. J. K. Fairbank (Chicago, 1957), pp. 132–62; and Heinrich Busch, "The Tun-lin Academy and Its Political and Philosophical Significance," *Monumenta Serica,* XIV (1949–55), 1–163.

45 This, if I do not distort it unduly in condensation, is the interpretation repeatedly advanced by Wolfram Eberhard. See, for example, his *Conquerors and Rulers: Social Forces in Medieval China* (Leiden, 1952).

46 This seems to be the view of Karl A. Wittfogel, as expounded in detail in his *op. cit.*

47 Some of the terminology here is borrowed from K. V. Rangaswami, as quoted in Wittfogel, *op. cit.*, p. 103.

48 Ku Chieh-kang, "A Study of Literary Persecution During the Ming," trans. L. C. Goodrich, *Harvard Journal of Asiatic Studies,* III (1938), 254–311.

49 See my article "Confucianism and the Chinese Censorial System," in *Confucianism in Action,* especially pp. 207–08.

50 G. A. Kennedy's biography of Chu Yü-chien in *Eminent Chinese of the Ch'ing Period,* ed. A. W. Hummel (Washington, 1943–44), I, 196–98.

51 Semedo, *op. cit.*, p. 122.

52 Wan Kuo-ting, "Ming-tai Chuang-t'ien K'ao-lüeh," *Chin-ling Hsüeh-pao,* III, Part 2 (November 1933), 295–310.

53 For the rebellion of the Prince of Han in 1425, see MS, chap. 118, pp. 16b–21a; for that of the Prince of Ning in 1519, see MS, chap. 117, pp. 16b ff. and Chang Yü-ch'uan, "Wang Shou-jen as a Statesman," *Chinese Social and Political Science Review,* XXIII (1939–40), 30–99, 155–259, 319–75, 473–517.

54 MS, chap. 113, pp. 1a-2a, chap. 300, pp. 1a-1b.
55 See MS, chaps. 113 and 300, *passim.*

[56] For some of the concepts and terms here I am indebted to Albin W. Gouldner, "Organizational Analysis," in *Sociology Today: Problems and Prospects,* ed. R. K. Merton et al (New York, 1959), pp. 400–28.

[57] Ricci, *op. cit.,* pp. 55–56.

[58] TMHT, chap. 80, p. 1834; Sun Ch'eng-tse, *Ch'un-ming Mengyü Lu* (Ku-hsiang chai ed.), chap. 48, pp. 65b–66a.

[59] *T'ai-tsu Shih-lu,* chap. 165, p. 3a.

[60] Ch'ien Mu, *Kuo-shih Ta-kang* (Taipei, 1952), II, 477.

[61] *Ibid.;* Hucker, "Confucianism and the Chinese Censorial System," *op. cit.,* pp. 199 ff.; and W. T. de Bary, "Chinese Despotism and the Confucian Ideal," in *Chinese Thought and Institutions,* pp. 174–75.

[62] de Bary, *op. cit.,* p. 174, reporting the views of Huang Tsung-hsi.

[63] E.g., see Hucker, "The Tung-lin Movement of the Late Ming Period," *op. cit.*

[64] For details on some aspects of the Ming censorial system, see my articles "The Traditional Chinese Censorate and the New Peking Regime," *American Political Science Review,* XLV (1951), 1041–1057; and "Confucianism and the Chinese Censorial System," *op. cit.*

[65] The discussion here is derived in large part from Hucker, "The Tung-lin Movement of the Late Ming Period," *op. cit.,* pp. 136 ff.

[66] See de Bary, *op cit.,* p. 175; cf. Ch'ien Mu, *Chung-kuo Li-tai Cheng-chih Te-shih* (Hongkong, 1952), pp. 79–85.

[67] See MS, chap. 74, pp. 24a–32a and chaps. 304–05; Ting I, *op. cit.;* Ch'ien Mu, *Kuo-shih Ta-kang,* II, 479–87.

[68] Cf. T. F. Tout, *The Collected Papers of Thomas Frederick Tout,* III (Manchester, 1934), chap. 7: "The English Civil Service in the Fourteenth Century," especially p. 202.

[69] Hucker, "The Tung-lin Movement of the Late Ming Period," *op. cit.,* p. 162. Cf. the views of Huang Tsung-hsi on eunuchs, summarized in de Bary, *op. cit.,* 176–77.

[70] See Ch'ien Mu, *Chung-kuo Li-tai Cheng-chih Te-shih,* pp. 92–95; and de Bary, *op. cit.,* pp. 184–86.

[71] The prescribed functions of the government are described in MS, chaps. 25–95. Cf. TMHT, *passim*.

[72] Ricci, *op. cit.*, pp. 54–55.

[73] See Liang Fang-chung, *op.cit.*

[74] *Ku-chin T'u-shu Chi-ch'eng* (photolithographic reproduction, 1934), Shih-huo Tien section, chap. 253 (vol. 696, pp. 24a–24b).

[75] *Hsü Wen-hsien T'ung-k'ao*, chap. 30, p. 3088.

[76] L. C. Goodrich, *A Short History of the Chinese People* (3d ed.; New York, 1959), p. 199.

[77] MS, chap. 93, pp. 4a–4b.

[78] C. R. Boxer, ed., *South China in the Sixteenth Century* (London, 1953), pp. 178–79.

[79] See my article "Su-chou and the Agents of Wei Chung-hsien: A Translation of K'ai-tu ch'uan-hsin," in *Silver Jubilee Volume of the Zinbun-Kagaku-Kenkyusyo* (Kyoto, 1954), pp. 224–56; and Ting I, *op. cit.*, *passim*.

[80] See Boxer, *op. cit.*, especially pp. 175–85.

[81] For example, see Hucker, "Su-chou and the Agents of Wei Chung-hsien," *op. cit.*, pp. 243 ff.

[82] For some examples during the generally peaceful reign of Hsüan-tsung, see *Hsüan-tsung Shih-lu* (photolithographic reproduction, 1940), chap. 89, p. 4b, chap. 59, p. 16b, chap. 98, p. 1a, and chap. 109, p. 12a.

[83] J. K. Shryock, *The Origin and Development of the State Cult of Confucius: An Introductory Study* (New York, 1932), p. 51.

[84] Wittfogel, *op. cit.*, p. 139.

[85] See Boxer, *op. cit.*, pp. 17, 175–85.

[86] Ricci, *op. cit.*, p. 81.

[87] For examples, see *Hsüan-tsung Shih-lu*, chap. 41, p. 13b, chap. 104, pp. 10a–10b.

[88] *Lun-yü* 2.3, trans. Arthur Waley, *The Analects of Confucius* (London, 1938), p. 88.

Lun-yü 12.19, trans. Waley, *op. cit.*, p. 168.

9023